MW01617011

Books in the Writers' Guide Series

Goal Setting for Writers
How to set and achieve your writing goals, write a book, and become a successful author

Time Management for Writers
How to write faster, find the time to write your book, and be a more prolific writer

Show, Don't Tell
How to write vivid descriptions, handle backstory, and describe your characters' emotions

Point of View
How to use the different POV types, avoid head-hopping, and choose the best point of view for your book

Write Great Beginnings
How to start a novel, hook readers from page one, and avoid common first-chapter problems

Write Great Beginnings

HOW TO

☑ START A NOVEL

☑ HOOK READERS FROM PAGE ONE

☑ AVOID COMMON FIRST-CHAPTER PROBLEMS

SANDRA GERTH

Table of Contents

PART I — Introduction

1. The importance of the opening — Why writing a great beginning is crucial

I have a feeling you already understand that the beginning of your book is important; otherwise, you probably wouldn't have bought this book. But the beginning isn't just important. It's *the most important* part of your book. Sure, it's essential to write a captivating middle and a satisfying ending too, but it's the opening that will make an editor decide to accept your manuscript for publication. Even if you're an indie author who self-publishes and doesn't have to impress agents or editors, writing a great beginning is still vital because you do have to impress readers as they buy or don't buy your book based on its opening.

Your opening is the first thing literary agents, acquisition editors, and readers will see of your story. They will judge your book and your writing skills in general based on the first few pages they read. This is your chance to make a good first impression. More often than not, you won't get another.

If your beginning is weak, it doesn't matter how brilliantly written the rest of your book is. Readers, agents, and editors will never find out about the clever plot twist in chapter 11, your action-packed showdown, or your moving ending because they will stop reading long before they get to the good parts.

YOUR BEGINNING IS A MARKETING TOOL

The first few pages of your book are actually a marketing tool. As award-winning crime novelist Mickey Spillane said, "The first chapter sells the book." Think about how readers make the decision to buy a book. For most readers, it goes like this: The cover or title of the book draws their attention, so they read the description, which is commonly called the *blurb*. If the blurb sounds interesting, they will usually open the book to the first page or, if they are shopping at an online bookstore, click on the sample. On most online retailer sites, that sample contains the first ten percent of the book, so that part of the story is especially crucial. If readers get to the end of the excerpt and find themselves hooked, they'll buy the book. If the beginning doesn't capture their attention, they'll move on and buy another book.

Nowadays, readers' attention spans are short. They won't patiently read several chapters, waiting around for something interesting to happen. You only have a page or two to convince readers to buy your book or editors to accept your manuscript.

BEGINNINGS ARE HARD TO WRITE

Yet many writers struggle to create a great opening for their book. Writing a riveting beginning is one of the hardest parts of the writing process for many authors. They agonize over their opening chapters; they rewrite, revise, and polish them over and over, without ever feeling completely satisfied with their story beginning.

Other writers are convinced they have written the perfect opening, only to be rejected by a literary agent or an editor or have the book not sell well.

If you are struggling with your opening chapters or are aiming to write a book that will be accepted by agents and publishers and eagerly bought by readers, this guide is for you.

WHAT THIS BOOK WILL TEACH YOU

As the senior editor of a small publishing house, I'm in charge of reading submissions and deciding what manuscripts are accepted for publication. We reject manuscripts for a lot of different reasons, but most of the time, it's because the opening failed to capture our interest or the writer committed one of the mistakes that are common in opening chapters: a beginning that is too slow, lacks conflict, or starts in the wrong place.

During the course of this book, I'll teach you how to avoid these mistakes and how to write an opening that will keep agents, editors, and readers reading.

Whether you're a novice writer working on your first book or an established author who has already published multiple novels, this guide will help you:

- Decide where to start your book
- Write a kickass first line
- Hook your readers from the very first page
- Avoid openings that are boring, clichéd, or misleading
- Decide whether opening your book with a prologue is a good idea
- Get your readers emotionally involved in your story as soon as possible
- Introduce your characters and your setting
- Pick a point of view and tense for your story
- Incorporate backstory and descriptions without stopping the momentum of your story

- Discover what types of openings to avoid
- Understand the three-act structure and the elements of the first act
- Create chapter endings that will make readers keep reading

HOW TO GET THE MOST OUT OF THIS BOOK

Each chapter of this book ends with practical exercises that will help you apply what you are learning to your own manuscript.

While you're reading this book, I suggest you stop after every chapter and do the exercises. I know it's tempting to skip this step, thinking you'll come back and do the exercises later, but if you are anything like me, you might be too busy to read the book a second time. So take the time to work on the exercises while everything is fresh in your mind.

Print out the first three chapters of your manuscript or set up a file in your favorite writing app, and do the exercises as you finish each chapter.

By the time you get to the end of this guide, I'm confident that you'll have a beginning that will hook agents, editors, and readers alike.

A NOTE ON THE EXAMPLES I USE

A few of the examples I use throughout this book are from my own novels, written under my pen name, Jae (https://jae-fiction.com). I do that not because I think my novels are the best ever but because I know them best, and I can quote from them as much as I want without violating anyone's copyright or humiliating a fellow writer for mistakes they've made.

I will also use examples not just from popular books but also from well-known movies. The same storytelling principles apply to both novels and movies, and I want to double my chances of you being familiar with some of the examples I'm using. If you haven't seen the movies or read the books and still want to do so, you might want to skip the example to avoid spoilers.

A NOTE ON PRONOUNS

Fiction is as diverse as life. You might be writing about a character who identifies as female, male, nonbinary, or something else entirely. Throughout this book, I'll use *they/them/their* as a singular, gender-neutral pronoun unless I'm talking about a specific character whose pronouns are *he/his* or *she/her*.

Happy reading and writing!
Sandra Gerth

EXERCISE #1:

- The next time you are looking for a book to read, browsing a bookstore, a library, or an online retailer's site, observe yourself. How much of a book do you read before you decide to buy or not buy it?

EXERCISE #2:

- Read your own manuscript up to the spot where you usually make your buying decision, e.g., the first page or the end of the first chapter. Try to view it objectively. If you were a reader coming across your book for the first time, would you buy it based on what you've read?

2. Definition —
What a story's beginning is

I think a book about beginnings needs to start at the beginning. Before we discuss what makes a great opening and what mistakes to avoid, we should talk about how we define the word *opening*.

WHAT CONSTITUTES THE BEGINNING?

What counts as a story's beginning? Is it the opening line? The first paragraph? The first page? The first scene? The first chapter? The first ten percent of a story, which is available to readers as a sample in most online bookstores? Or maybe the first three chapters, which is usually what literary agents and acquisition editors request?

There's no clear rule as to what constitutes the beginning, but I'd say yes to all of the above. In most stories, all of these things are part of the beginning, so we'll discuss everything from the first line to the first three chapters. Depending on your book, we might even go beyond the first three chapters.

The opening of your novel can take up as much as 25 percent of the book, which would mean 20,000 words of an 80,000-word novel.

DEFINITION OF *BEGINNING*

The beginning is the setup of a story—the part where the main characters and the story world are introduced to the reader, along with the major problem or conflict that the protagonist will spend the rest of the book trying to solve. Usually, all of that happens within the first three chapters of a book, but depending on the length of your novel and your chapters, your opening might consist of just two chapters or as many as four to five chapters.

The beginning starts with the very first word of the story and ends with the protagonist's commitment to their story goal. For example, the detective accepts the case in a murder mystery, Katniss volunteers as a tribute in *The Hunger Games* by Suzanne Collins, and Luke Skywalker decides to accompany Obi-Wan Kenobi to Alderaan and join the rebellion in *Star Wars: Episode IV – A New Hope*.

Whether you write epic fantasy, a fast-paced thriller, or a romance, this guide will take you all the way from the first line to the end of your story's beginning.

EXERCISE #3:

• Re-read the opening chapters of your three favorite novels in the genre you write. Where would you say the beginning ends? How far into the book are you? Is it the same for all three books?

EXERCISE #4:

• Now take a look at your own work-in-progress or novel. Where does your beginning end? How far into the story are you?

3. First drafts and revisions —
Why you don't have to get it perfect right away

After everything I've told you about the importance of your story opening, you might feel a little worried, intimidated, or stressed because there's so much riding on your opening. All that pressure might even keep you from finishing your manuscript—or from starting it in the first place.

WRITING ISN'T BRAIN SURGERY

But I've got good news for you: Writing isn't brain surgery. You don't have to get it right on your first try. Don't worry too much about writing the perfect opening during your first draft. Every experienced writer knows that the real magic happens during the revision process. Write your opening chapters, but resist the urge to rewrite and polish them for months before you move on. You can always come back later, after you finish the first draft, and revise whatever isn't working.

THE FIRST DRAFT IS FOR DISCOVERY, NOT PERFECTION

During the first-draft stage, all that matters is getting the words onto the page. They don't have to be perfect. For many writers, the first draft is about discovering the story and getting to know their characters.

You will probably find out some new things about your characters as you write the first draft. The story will take some unexpected turns, and by the time you reach the end of the book, the beginning you wrote months ago might not be a good fit for the story anymore.

That's the reason it's easier to decide on how to open your book once you know how your book is going to end. You'll then be able to recognize what needs to be changed in your opening chapters. You might even end up cutting an entire scene or chapter. In one of my novels, *Just Physical*, I cut the first two chapters during the revision process and decided to open the book with chapter 3. If I had spent months agonizing over every single word and every comma in those first two chapters, I would have ended up wasting a lot of time. Just get the opening written to the best of your ability and then move on and come back to it later.

IF IT HELPS, SKIP THE BEGINNING

If you find the beginning of your book hard to write, you could even skip writing the opening scene or the opening chapter and start with chapter two or a scene later in the book. The beginning is the first thing your readers will read, but it doesn't necessarily have to be the first thing you write. For some writers, the first chapter is actually the last thing they write. If writing out of chronological order works for you, you could just put in a placeholder such as *[insert amazing opening scene here]* and move on. Once you finish the book, the perfect way to start the story should be easier to judge.

EXERCISE #5:

• Reflect on what kind of writer you are. Would it help you get started if you skipped the opening chapter and wrote it later? Or do you work best if you write in a chronological order, starting at the very beginning and then coming back later to revise the first chapter? If you're not sure, give both a try, and see what works best for you.

PART II —
Milestones of a great beginning

Like the start of any interesting journey, the beginning of a novel, a novella, or even a short story has milestones—certain points your readers expect you to hit to make the trip satisfying for them.

In this part, I'll teach you all about those milestones and give you a roadmap that will help you take your readers on a journey they're sure to enjoy.

4. The three-act structure —
How understanding story structure can help your writing

If you've read any other books or blogs on writing, you have probably heard of the three-act structure. It's the most commonly used story structure, and it has been around since the times of Aristotle.

I can almost hear some of you groan at the term *structure*. Won't using a template like the three-act structure make your writing formulaic?

No. We're talking about a very broad pattern that makes stories work, not a rigid, overly detailed plan that would limit your creativity. Basically, the three-act structure says that all stories consist of three parts:

- **A beginning (act 1):** Act 1 is also called the **setup**. It introduces the main characters, the setting, and the situation. Then something happens that changes the protagonist's life and makes them decide to pursue a goal.

- **A middle (act 2):** Act 2 is also called the **confrontation**. The main character works toward their goal but faces escalating obstacles, forcing them to learn and grow.

- **An end (act 3):** Act 3 is called the **resolution**. The main character either fails or achieves their goal. In most novels, the protagonist will succeed with the help of the lessons they have learned along the way.

That's a natural pattern, not just for novels, but also for movies and episodes of TV shows. Even this nonfiction guide has a beginning (part I, the introduction), a middle (which begins with this chapter), and an end (the conclusion).

Most stories, consciously or unconsciously, follow this pattern, and they have done so for thousands of years. It holds a universal appeal to us humans, maybe because so many things in our lives—even life itself— have a beginning, a middle, and an end. For example, each day consists of a morning, an afternoon, and an evening. A roller coaster ride starts with the initial climb, is followed by the twists and turns, and then concludes when the cars slide to a stop. Using the same structure for your stories gives readers the familiar framework they need to relax and enjoy the ride.

In most novels, the first and the third act each take up about 25 percent of the story, while the second act makes up the middle 50 percent of the book. Sometimes, the middle is further divided into two acts, separated by the midpoint. That results in a four-act structure, with each act taking up about a quarter of the story.

PLOTTER, PANTSER, OR SOMEWHERE IN BETWEEN

"Wait a minute," some of you might say. What if you're still not comfortable with all that talk of *structure*? All you wanted was to write a captivating beginning, and suddenly we're talking about acts, structure, and how much space each part of the story is supposed to take up.

For some of you, it might feel stifling to think about things like that during the first draft of your manuscript.

As you might know, writers are often divided into two groups: plotters and pantsers.

Plotters are outline writers who plot out the story in advance. They often spend a considerable amount of time planning, creating an outline, and doing character sketches before they start to write.

Pantsers—also referred to as organic writers or discovery writers—are people who write by the seat of their pants instead of outlining the book. They start with no or only a vague idea of where the story might end up and figure it all out as they go along. If they mapped out their story ahead of time, they would feel constrained and might even lose interest because for them discovering the story and the characters as they go is half the fun.

I'm not going to tell you that one of these approaches is superior to the other. Plotting and pantsing both have their advantages and disadvantages. There's no right or wrong way to write a book—there's just the right way for you.

Most writers don't fall firmly into one category or the other anyway. It's more helpful to think of plotting vs. pantsing as a continuum, with most writers falling somewhere in between.

Personally, I'm a hybrid too—a plantser, if you will. I plot my books before I begin writing, but my outline isn't overly detailed. I usually know the major plot points but figure out all the little events between them as I go.

Find out what works for you, and don't be afraid to experiment and adjust your process accordingly.

HOW PANTSERS CAN BENEFIT FROM THIS SECTION

I firmly believe that understanding the three-act structure can still help you, even if you are a pantser.

First of all, being familiar with structure will keep you on track and might save you from having your story meander all over the place. Even if you don't yet know what will happen in your story, being aware of the underlying universal patterns and elements of storytelling will guide you in the right direction. Your subconscious will shape the story around important plot points even without you consciously thinking about structure.

Secondly, you don't necessarily need to use your knowledge of story structure during the first draft. You could use the three-act structure to analyze and revise your story after you finish the first draft. Does your story have all the major plot points, and do they happen at roughly the right time? Does the first turning point happen too late, making the beginning seem to drag? Is your ending rushed?

No matter where you fall on the plotter-pantser continuum, you can benefit from studying the following chapters closely.

I'll focus on act 1 because this is a guide on writing great beginnings. If you need some help with act 2 and 3, here are a few book recommendations:

- *Structuring Your Novel: Essential Keys for Writing an Outstanding Story* by K.M. Weiland
- *Save the Cat!: The Last Book on Screenwriting You'll Ever Need* by Blake Snyder
- *Save the Cat! Writes a Novel* by Jessica Brody

- *The Writer's Journey: Mythic Structure for Writers* by Christopher Vogler
- *The Plot Whisperer: Secrets of Story Structure Any Writer Can Master* by Martha Alderson

So let's take a closer look at the topic of this book: act 1, which is the beginning of a story.

FUNCTION AND LENGTH OF ACT 1

The function of the first act is to introduce your main characters, your story world, and the main conflict.

As I mentioned earlier, the beginning usually takes up about 25 percent of the story, which would be the first 20,000 words of an 80,000-word novel. However, nowadays, openings are often shorter, so it might actually only comprise 15 to 20 percent (12,000-16,000 words).

Consider this number as a rough guideline, not something set in stone. The length of a novel's opening varies depending on the individual book and its genre. Fast-paced thrillers and mysteries often have shorter openings, while the beginning of an epic fantasy novel might take up more pages. You do have a bit of leeway, but don't overdo it. If your first act takes up a third of your book, it could become tedious, and your readers are likely to get bored.

PARTS OF ACT 1

The first act consists of four important components:

1. The ordinary world
2. The inciting incident

3. The refusal of the call
4. The point of no return

If you have never heard of these plot milestones, don't worry. We'll take a closer look at each of them in the next chapters.

EXERCISE #6:

- Where on the plotter-pantser continuum do you fall?
- How does that influence your handling of story structure? At what point of your writing process would you take a closer look at your story's structure—during the plotting stage, during the revision process, or somewhere along the way?

5. The ordinary world —
How to introduce your protagonist's normal life

The first scene of a book often introduces what Christopher Vogler in *The Writer's Journey* calls the protagonist's *ordinary world*.

It's a quick snapshot of the main character and their status quo before something happens to change everything. What does life look like for your main character before the inciting incident?

For example, *Harry Potter and the Philosopher's Stone* (or *Harry Potter and the Sorcerer's Stone*, for the US edition) by J.K. Rowling opens with a few pages describing Harry's life with the Dursleys and how he came to live with them.

GOALS OF THE ORDINARY WORLD SCENE

In this part of the story, you should have at least three—and sometimes four—goals in mind:

- **Introduce the main character(s):** Show readers what kind of person your protagonist is. What are their most important personality traits? What flaws do they have? What are their goals at the moment? Notice that I said show, not tell them about your main character. Instead of telling your readers "Julia was a kind woman," show her paying for another customer who finds himself a few dollars short at the checkout. For example, the ordinary world section of the movie Finding Nemo does a good job introducing Marlin's personality traits and flaws: After losing his wife and all the other eggs, he's an overprotective father who is scared of taking risks. If you want to find out more about how to show instead of tell, check out my writers' guide *Show, Don't Tell*. Depending on when you are reading this book, *Show, Don't Tell* might even be available for free.

- **Build a connection:** Get the reader to connect and sympathize with your main character so that they will actually care when the inciting incident changes their life completely. This connection between protagonist and readers is what will keep them turning the pages to find out what happens to the character. If readers aren't emotionally invested in your characters, they won't care whether they achieve their goals and get their desired endings. Chapter 11 of this guide will tell you all about how to create that important connection.

- **Provide context and contrast:** The ordinary world scene gives readers an understanding of the protagonist's normal life so they will then realize when things change and understand why the inciting incident is so disturbing to the character. For example, in my romance novel *Just for Show*, I felt readers needed a glimpse into the main character's personality before the inciting incident hit. After realizing how much of a perfectionist Claire is, they understood better why the inciting incident—her fiancée breaking up with her—hit her especially hard because it destroyed Claire's image of having the perfect life. The ordinary world also gives us a baseline for who the main character is at the beginning of the story, including their fears and flaws. That starting point of the character arc will provide a contrast with how far they have come in the final scene.

- **Mirror the final scene.** In some books, the opening scene is a mirror of the very last scene—with one important difference. This is also called a circular ending. The main character might be in a very similar situation in the first and the last scene, but they'll act differently because the events of the book have changed them forever. For example, my romance novel *Not the Marrying Kind* starts and ends with a scene that takes place in a bakery, where the main character buys a cupcake. But in the opening scene, she makes the safe choice, a vanilla cupcake, while she chooses a decadent chocolate one with salted caramel frosting in the final scene. It might seem like a small difference, but readers who've read the book will understand the fundamental change it symbolizes.

THE PROBLEM OF THE ORDINARY WORLD

The problem with this part of the story is that watching your characters do everyday things can get boring for readers very quickly, and a boring opening is the last thing you want. Here are some tips on how to avoid that problem:

- **Keep this part of the story short.** Show readers just enough of the ordinary world to give them a bit of context and get them to bond with the main character before you have the inciting incident happen. It doesn't even need to be a full scene. Depending on the story, a few paragraphs can be enough.

- **Make the ordinary world interesting, not mundane.** Don't show your protagonist waking up, brushing their teeth, and having breakfast. Make sure you don't bore readers with your character's everyday routine.

- **Hint that something is about to happen** and this is just the calm before the storm. Something unusual is starting to happen. In *The*

Hunger Games by Suzanne Collins, we learn that this is the day of the reaping.

- **Raise questions.** Make sure your first scene includes things that spark questions in readers' minds. In *The Hunger Games* by Suzanne Collins, we immediately want to know what exactly the reaping is. We read on to find out what the reaping is and whose names will be drawn. (In case you're unfamiliar with the book, the reaping is an annual event where the tributes for the Hunger Games are chosen.) I'll explain more about how to raise questions in readers' minds in a later chapter.

- **Give the main character a goal right away.** It doesn't need to be the big story goal that they'll pursue throughout the rest of the book, but make them want *something*. Active characters that go after a goal are always more interesting than passive ones.

- **Show your protagonist dealing with a conflict or problem.** The way they handle problems will show your readers a lot about their personality. For example, in my novel *Not the Marrying Kind*, florist Ashley is confronted with a customer who's buying expensive roses for his mistress, while telling Ashley to make up a bunch of "whatever" for his wife. Instead of calling him out or telling his wife about the affair, she sends him home with a bouquet of flowers where, unbeknownst to most people, each flower she has chosen symbolizes deception and disloyalty. Not only does that bit of tension keep the scene of Ashley selling flowers from being boring, it also shows us that she's someone who doesn't deal with conflict head-on.

- **Reveal your character's flaw, fear, or misguided belief.** Give readers at least a hint of the protagonist's character arc—the life lesson they'll have to learn or flaw they'll have to overcome by the end of the book if they want to succeed, even if they don't know it yet. Show that something has to change. The status quo can't go on because the flaw negatively affects the character's life and keeps them from true happiness, even if they think they're content. For example, in the opening scene of my romance novel *Just for Show*, main character Claire is putting the finishing touches on the buffet for her engagement party, even though she hired a catering service. Readers are introduced to her flaw: she's too much of a perfectionist and micromanages everything, which is one of the reasons her fiancée breaks up with her later in the same scene.

EXERCISE #7:

- Take a look at your top three favorite novels in your chosen genre. How much of the protagonist's everyday world do they show before the inciting incident happens? How does the author keep the ordinary world from being boring?

EXERCISE #8:

- If you are already in the revision stage of your novel, take a look at your opening scene. How much of your protagonist's everyday world are you showing? Do you need to cut some of it to avoid it dragging? Or do you need to show a little bit more of the everyday world to provide context for the inciting incident?
- If you are still planning your story, think about how you want to open your book. How much of the character's everyday life do you want to show? How will you keep it from becoming boring?

EXERCISE #9:

- Go over the "goals of the ordinary world scene" section in this chapter, and use it as a checklist. Does your ordinary world scene achieve at least the first three of these goals? If not, how could you achieve these goals?

EXERCISE #10:

- Go over the "problem of the ordinary world" section above, and use it as a checklist. Does your story opening do all these things? If not, can you think of ways to revise it?

6. The inciting incident —
How to set your plot in motion

So you've established your character's ordinary world. But, of course, you can't have the everyday-life section go on forever. Readers will quickly grow bored because no real change is happening. Something needs to disrupt that status quo, force the character out of their comfort zone, and get the story going.

That something is the inciting incident. It's also referred to as the *call to adventure* (Christopher Vogler), *the disturbance*, or *the catalyst* (Blake Snyder). It's an event or trigger that kicks the story into motion after you've introduced the character's ordinary world. Even though the protagonist might not realize it right away, that event will force them out of their ordinary world and change their life forever.

TWO TYPES OF INCITING INCIDENTS

There are two forms of inciting incidents. The inciting incident can present itself either as a problem the character has to deal with or as an opportunity to improve their life.

Most stories have a **problem inciting incident**, where something bad happens to the protagonist: the main character is fired from their job, their child is kidnapped, they are falsely accused of murder, or they get stuck in an elevator with their arch enemy.

But the inciting incident could also be a positive event or an **opportunity** that presents itself to the character, e.g., the character wins ten million dollars in the lottery. Usually, that opportunity comes with a catch.

They have a choice to make that promises a great reward but that also comes with a cost or risk. For example, in my romance novel *Not the Marrying Kind*, Ashley is offered a chance to make peace with her ex-girlfriend and get their friendship back—but in order to do that, she has to do the flowers for a lesbian wedding, knowing that her parents and the conservative town won't like it.

EXAMPLES FOR INCITING INCIDENTS

- *The Hunger Games* by Suzanne Collins: Katniss witnesses the name of her younger sister, Prim, being drawn to be tribute, which means Prim will have to fight in the Hunger Games.

- *Star Wars: Episode IV – A New Hope*: Luke Skywalker receives Princess Leia's holographic message.

- *Harry Potter and the Philosopher's Stone* (or *Harry Potter and the Sorcerer's Stone*, for the US edition) by J.K. Rowling: Harry receives a letter of acceptance to Hogwarts School of Witchcraft and Wizardry.

- *The Martian* by Andy Weir: A sandstorm hits and the crew leaves Mark behind for dead, so now he's stranded on Mars, alone.

- In my romance novel *Perfect Rhythm,* Leo gets a call from her estranged mother, telling her to come home because her father had a stroke.

- *Finding Nemo*: Clown fish Marlin is forced to watch as his son, Nemo, is captured by scuba divers.

- *Tootsie*: Out-of-work actor Michael finds out from his agent that no one in Hollywood will ever hire him again because he's difficult to work with.

THE INCITING INCIDENT AND YOUR GENRE

The catalyst that kicks off the story is often genre-specific, meaning it will be influenced by the genre of the book you're writing.

- **In a romance novel**, the inciting incident is often (but not always) the first time the two future lovers meet or, if they already know each other, the first time they are on the page together. Sometimes, that scene is referred to as the "meet cute" because in old romantic comedies the characters would often meet in a cute, funny way, e.g., literally running into each other. In some romance novels, the inciting incident is a separate event which leads to their first meeting. It's the domino that sets the romantic arc into motion by getting the characters onto the page together. For example, in *A Heart This Big* by Cheyenne Blue, the inciting incident is seven-year-old Billy falling off a horse and his mother suing, which leads to the farm owner, Nina, contacting a lawyer, who turns out to be her love interest.

- **In a thriller**, the inciting incident is often an attack by the villain.

- **In a mystery or crime novel**, the inciting incident is usually a crime being committed or discovered, e.g., a dead body is found, or a client approaching a private investigator with a new case.

MUST-DO'S OF THE INCITING INCIDENT

To be effective, an inciting incident needs to do several things. If you have two (or more) main characters, the inciting incident should accomplish these things for all of them.

- **It kicks off the story.** The inciting incident is what triggers the plot into motion. Without it, the rest of the book wouldn't happen. For example, in *The Lord of the Rings* by J.R.R. Tolkien, the inciting incident is Frodo's uncle leaving behind the ring for Frodo. If the ring hadn't come into Frodo's possession, he wouldn't have set out on his adventures in an attempt to destroy it. If your inciting incident is unrelated to the rest of your plot, go back and pick another catalyst.

- **It needs to be big enough** to force the protagonist's life in a new direction and change it forever.

- **It needs to push the protagonist out of their comfort zone** and trigger their flaws and fears. Throughout the course of the novel, the new situation will force them to confront those flaws and fears and to slowly change. For example, in my romance novel *Perfect Rhythm*, Leo hates small-town life and, as a result, left her hometown when she was eighteen. When her mother calls and tells her to come home, that triggers all the old feelings of not fitting in and being the subject of gossip. At first, she hates being back, but over the course of the novel, she slowly starts to see positive things about living in a small town.

- **It needs to happen on the page.** Readers need to witness it happen, so you can't let it happen "off-screen" and then only tell readers about it in the form of backstory afterward.

- **It needs to happen *to* the protagonist**. The inciting incident is usually brought on by someone else, not by the main character.

- **It needs to cause an emotional reaction in the protagonist**. It can't be a neutral event; it has to be something that causes strong emotions—positive or negative—in the main character, and you have to dip into your character's point of view and share some of those emotions with your readers.

- **It needs to create an external goal for the main character**. The inciting incident either offers your protagonist an opportunity or it throws their life out of balance and their goal will be to restore that balance. For example, in *A Heart This Big* by Cheyenne Blue, the inciting incident threatens the existence of Nina's farm, so it creates a goal for her: saving the farm by hiring the best lawyer possible.

PLACEMENT OF THE INCITING INCIDENT

So where in your story should your inciting incident happen? Screenwriting guides will usually tell you that it needs to land at the 10 to 12 percent mark, which means halfway through your first act, but this number isn't set in stone.

Generally speaking, the inciting incident should happen as soon as possible. For many novels, that will mean within the first chapter, but definitely not after the third.

In a lot of the manuscripts I edit, the inciting incident happens too late in the book. Many novice writers start their story in the wrong place and spend the first three chapters introducing the characters and describing the setting, without anything really happening. If that problem isn't addressed in the revision phase, readers might feel that the beginning is too slow and lose interest. So my advice would be to keep the ordinary world section short.

Some editors and writing coaches will even tell you to skip the ordinary world entirely and start the story with the inciting incident. That's a good choice for some books, but not for others. Where to place your inciting incident and how to start depends on your individual book. For some books, the best place to start is at the moment of change, while for others, it's right before that moment.

For example, in *The Hunger Games* by Suzanne Collins, the inciting incident—Prim's name being drawn as a tribute—happens on page 17. We need those first 17 pages to understand a little of Katniss's world. We learn that their father died, so Katniss took over the role of protector to her family. We need that information to understand why her sister's name being drawn disturbs her world so much and why she would be willing to risk her own life by volunteering in her place.

In comparison, *The Martian* by Andy Weir opens with the main character already in trouble, stranded alone on Mars. The author chose not to show how the protagonist was picked for the mission. He also didn't describe the journey to Mars. We don't need to have any of that information to understand that being left behind, presumed dead, on a planet with limited supplies, is a very bad thing.

Keep the ordinary world section as short as possible, yet as long as necessary. What does that mean? How much of the character's ordinary world you decide to reveal should depend on the nature of your inciting incident. Is it an event that readers would understand without any or much context, as in *The Martian*? Or would the inciting incident have more impact if you showed readers a little context and gave them some time to bond with your main character first, as in *The Hunger Games*?

Ask yourself how much the reader needs to know about the main characters and their lives in order to understand what the inciting incident means to them. In most cases, readers don't need to know as much as you think they do, so don't start too far back. Remember that you can always fill in some details about the characters' lives later in the story. I'll give you some helpful tips on how to do that in part IV of this guide.

Whether you'll have an ordinary world section might also depend on the genre of your book. Fast-paced thrillers or crime novels will usually begin with the inciting incident—usually a crime being committed or discovered. It's not uncommon to have a dead body on the very first page in a mystery. In contrast, a historical fiction, science fiction, or fantasy novel will usually spend a bit of time introducing the story world.

Your goal is to find the right balance for your story. Don't place the inciting incident so late that your readers will become impatient, but don't have it happen right away if that would confuse readers because they are missing all the context.

WHAT IF YOU HAVE TWO PROTAGONISTS?

But what if your story has two protagonists, as romance novels usually do? Do you need two ordinary world sections and two inciting incidents, one for each main character?

First of all, even if you have two main characters, they often won't be equally important. You might spend more time in one character's point of view. Usually, this is the character who will change more over the course of the story and who'll have to overcome more profound fears and flaws. If that's the case, this will be your main protagonist, so to say. Opening the book in that character's point of view might be a good idea, and if you have an ordinary world section, it will usually be the ordinary world of this character. If necessary, you can fill in some details about the other main character's life later in the book.

If both main characters are equally important, you could give readers glimpses of the ordinary worlds of both main characters. The first scene (or sometimes the entire first chapter) could show main character 1 in their world, while the second scene (or chapter) introduces main character 2 and their ordinary world. The third scene (or chapter) will then have them meet for the first time. If you do it that way, make sure you keep the ordinary world sections short so you don't delay the inciting incident—their first meeting.

Unless you have a strong subplot that requires its own inciting incident, your story will usually have only *one* inciting incident, though. It's often the moment the paths of your main characters collide or the event that triggers their first meeting.

Let me give you two examples from my own works to show you how multiple ordinary world sections can work together with one inciting incident.

I opened my romance novel *Not the Marrying Kind* with a scene showing one of the main characters, Sasha, in her bakery. The next scene shows the second main character, Ashley, in her flower shop. The inciting incident happens at the end of the first chapter, when they both find out that they are going to have to work together on a wedding. The structure of this opening is: ordinary world 1 — ordinary world 2 — inciting incident.

My romance novel *The Roommate Arrangement* opens with the ordinary world of Steph, a comedian trying to find an apartment near the comedy clubs in LA. When she hears about an apartment that is situated in the perfect location, it comes with a catch: the landlord doesn't rent to singles. That is the inciting incident, because it leads her to look for a roommate willing to pose as her fake romantic partner—which leads her to Rae, a doorwoman at an LA comedy club who is also looking for an apartment. When Steph first meets Rae, the scene shows a little of Rae's ordinary world. So the structure of the novel's beginning is: ordinary world 1 — inciting incident — ordinary world 2.

EXERCISE #11:

- Take a look at your top three favorite novels in your genre. Can you pinpoint the inciting incident for each of them? Does the story start with the inciting incident, or do we get an ordinary world section? Can you learn anything from how each author wrote the inciting incident and where they placed it?

EXERCISE #12:

- Now take a look at your own story. What's your inciting incident? Does it meet all the criteria for what an inciting incident should do? If not, how can you revise your inciting incident? Where did you place the inciting incident? Did you delay it for too long? If you did, tighten whatever comes before to the bare minimum readers need to understand the impact of the catalyst. Is your inciting incident strong enough to change the main character's life forever?
- If you are still in the planning stages of your novel: Do you feel it's necessary to show readers a bit of the character's ordinary world, or will you start the book with the inciting incident? What will your inciting incident be? Is it an event that meets all the criteria listed above? If not, can you revise it to meet all the must-do's or would it be better to pick another inciting incident?

7. The refusal of the call —
How to have your protagonist react to the inciting incident

In the previous plot milestone, your main character received the *call to adventure*, which introduces a big change in their life. But most people are creatures of habit and don't like change. So more often than not, the protagonist refuses the call to action and tries to cling to their ordinary world. For example, in *Star Wars: Episode IV – A New Hope*, Luke initially refuses to follow Obi-Wan and join the rebellion.

That's why this plot point is called the *refusal of the call* in Christopher Vogler's *The Writer's Journey*.

Most of us are scared of change, especially any kind of change that confronts us with our fears and weaknesses, and that's exactly what the inciting incident usually does. So instead of seizing the opportunity that presents itself in the inciting incident, the main character ignores the implications of whatever happened and tries to continue living their life the way it was before. They might try to deny there's a problem, or they might insist that it's not their problem to tackle. Sometimes, the protagonist tries to fix the problem in ways that don't work, trying to avoid the option that scares them.

Having a refusal of the call will make your character more real and human to readers. Readers will sympathize with a character who is plagued by fears, insecurities, and self-doubts in the face of a difficult challenge. They'll root for a protagonist who takes on the challenge despite their fears.

MUST-DO'S OF THE REFUSAL OF THE CALL

To be effective, the refusal of the call needs to do several things:

- **It needs to show the main character's emotional reaction to the inciting incident.** Whatever your inciting incident is, it's *big*. Your character might try to ignore it outwardly, but deep down, they need to react to it. For example, in my novel *Damage Control*, my protagonist, Grace, is angry when she finds out her mother fired her old publicist and hired a new one to deal with her newest PR nightmare.

- **It needs to show readers that the protagonist is reluctant to change because of a fear or flaw** they will have to overcome during the course of the book. You probably know the saying "nothing worth having is ever easy," and that's what your main character should experience in your story too. The plot should confront them with the hardest, scariest thing they have ever done—either physically or emotionally—so they are hesitant to take it on. If the protagonist felt competent to take on the challenge at the beginning of the story, there would be no tension and no room for growth. Make the challenge presented in the inciting incident a difficult, maybe even scary one for your protagonist. That doesn't mean that your character will have to climb Mount Everest or capture a dangerous killer. The inciting incident could present them with a goal that could be easy for someone else; it just needs to be hard for your protagonist because of their personal history.

- **It needs to reveal more about the main character's personality.** How does your protagonist deal with problems? Do they ignore it? Try to get someone else to deal with it? Try solutions that obviously won't work? Do they panic or stay calm under pressure?

DEBATE VS. REFUSAL

Is it always necessary for your protagonist to refuse the call to action? I don't think it is. In some stories, it makes no sense for the character to hesitate before accepting the call. For example, if your main character's family is taken hostage, and they're a police officer, they probably won't hesitate to take on the villain.

In books like that, the refusal of the call is more of a *debate*, as Blake Snyder calls this plot point in his screenwriting book *Save the Cat*.

The protagonist might experience self-doubts and wonder if they really have what it takes to master the challenge, but there's never a question whether they'll act or not. The debate might then be a period in which the protagonist doesn't know how to react or reacts emotionally to the inciting incident, without a real plan. For example, when Marlin's son is taken by divers in *Finding Nemo*, Marlin immediately swims after the boat. But when he can't keep up, he has no idea how to find Nemo. His goal—crossing the open sea to go after Nemo—only forms when he meets Dory and they find the diver's mask that tells them Nemo is in Sydney.

In some books, the debate isn't even much of a debate because the next step is pretty clear. For example, in *The Hunger Games* by Suzanne Collins, Katniss doesn't hesitate to volunteer as tribute in her sister's place, and she doesn't have much choice but to take the train to the capital to fight in the Hunger Games. So her internal debate is more about her wondering whether she'll be able to survive and whether she'll have the fortitude to kill another human. But we still get the three must-do's of the refusal plot point: we see Katniss's emotional reaction, we learn about her fear and self-doubts, and we find out more about her personality—for example, she doesn't cry, unlike the other character chosen as a tribute, Peeta.

LENGTH OF THE REFUSAL

Depending on your book, the refusal of the call could be just a short moment of hesitation that takes up only a few lines or it could be a longer period where the character works through a number of doubts and tries to ignore the problem, drawn out over several scenes. It all depends on your character's personality, their situation, and how unsettling taking on the goal triggered by the inciting incident is for them.

THE REFUSAL IN A ROMANCE NOVEL

While it's usually easy to identify the refusal of the call in a more plot-driven novel such as an adventure story or a fantasy novel, romance authors sometimes struggle to find this plot point in their manuscripts.

Basically, what the characters in a romance novel are refusing is love. During the inciting incident—usually their first meeting—there will often be a spark of attraction. Something about the other person captures their interest. However, it will usually be an unwanted attraction. They don't necessarily need to dislike or hate each other, but they aren't interested in falling in love, either in general or with each other.

Like in any other type of book, the reason for that refusal has to do with their fear or flaw. For example, in my romance novel *Just for Show*, perfectionist Claire doesn't want to fall in love with tattooed, chaotic, out-of-work actress Lana.

EXERCISE #13:

- Take another look at the three novels you analyzed in exercise 11. How do the characters react to the inciting incident? Can you identify a refusal of the call? How long does it go on for? What can you learn from the way these authors handled the refusal of the call?

EXERCISE #14:

- Now take a look at your own manuscript. Can you pinpoint a refusal of the call in your story? How long does it go on for, especially compared to the three novels you've just analyzed? Does it go on for too long? Or do you need to dive more deeply into your protagonist's emotional reaction and show more of their fears and flaws?

- If you are still planning your story, think about how your protagonist will react to the inciting incident. What kind of emotion will they feel? How can you *show* readers that emotion? Will your character hesitate to answer the call to adventure, and how long will that refusal go on for?

8. The point of no return — How to thrust your character into act 2

The inciting incident is the event that rocks the protagonist's world and introduces change, but usually, they refuse the call to action. In the section that is called *point of no return*, the protagonist gives up their resistance and accepts the call to action. Christopher Vogler refers to this plot point as *crossing the first threshold*, while Blake Snyder calls it *break into two* because it's the end of act 1 and launches the characters into act 2.

This plot point is also called *the first turning point* because it pushes the story in a new direction. The main character finally accepts the call to adventure and commits to the goal the inciting incident introduced.

In some books, something happens between the refusal of the call and the point of no return that increases the stakes and convinces the main character to stop ignoring the problem and take action. In other novels, an encouraging friend convinces them, or they work through their self-doubts on their own and decide they are ready to tackle the new adventure.

Whatever it is that makes the main character finally commit to their new goal, it needs to be irreversible. From here on out, there's no way back. Stories need that point of no return because the middle of the book will confront the main character with things that are way out of their comfort zone. We need something to keep them from just walking away and saying "never mind" when they encounter obstacles and are confronted with things that scare them. Without that point of no return, readers would find it unrealistic for the character to remain in the situation, or they could doubt that the conflict is challenging enough for the main character. After all, how bad could it be if the character stays in the situation without having to?

So make sure that after the point of no return, the character can't just give up on their goal, at least not without grave consequences.

EXAMPLES FOR POINTS OF NO RETURN

- *The Hunger Games* by Suzanne Collins: Katniss volunteers as tribute so her sister doesn't have to fight in the Hunger Games.

- *Star Wars: Episode IV – A New Hope*: Luke finds out that his aunt and uncle have been killed by stormtroopers, so he decides to go with Obi-Wan Kenobi to learn the ways of the Force and join the rebellion.

- *Harry Potter and the Philosopher's Stone* (or *Harry Potter and the Sorcerer's Stone*, for the US edition) by J.K. Rowling: Harry gets on the train to Hogwarts.

- *Finding Nemo*: Despite his fear of the open sea, Marlin decides to go after his son, Nemo.

- *Tootsie*: Michael auditions as Dorothy Michaels and gets the part.

- *Backwards to Oregon* by my alter ego, Jae: Nora decides to marry a perfect stranger and join a wagon train to Oregon.

THE POINT OF NO RETURN AND YOUR GENRE

Like the inciting incident, the point of no return will often be influenced by the genre of the book you're writing.

- In a **romance novel**, you need to come up with a reason why the two main characters will have to keep interacting throughout the story and can't walk away from each other, no matter what. That's why the point of no return is also called the *lock-in* or the *crucible*—it's the situation that keeps the characters together even as the conflict between them heats up and triggers all their fears. In romance novels, the crucible is often contained in the trope. For example, in a fake-relationship romance like my novel *Just for Show*, it's the fake relationship that keeps them together. In office romances, the characters have to work together, so neither can just leave whenever they want to.

- In a **mystery novel**, the first turning point is usually the protagonist accepting the case and committing to solving the crime. For example, chapter 1 of *A Trouble of Fools* by Linda Barnes ends with private investigator Carlotta Carlyle agreeing to look for her client's missing brother.

- In a **fantasy novel**, the first turning point is usually when the main character decides to embark on their quest. This often means that they go on a physical journey, so act 2 will likely take place in a setting different from where act 1 took place.

MUST-DO'S OF THE POINT OF NO RETURN

To be effective, the point of no return needs to do several things:

- **It needs to truly be a point of no return.** After the first turning point, it needs to be impossible for the protagonist to just walk away and return to their ordinary world. The decision they are making should burn all bridges.

- **It needs to show the character's commitment to their goal.** Despite any earlier reluctance, the main character now needs to be fully committed to the story goal. Make sure you give your protagonist a strong motivation for reaching that goal. Something personal needs to be at stake for the main character. Without it, the book won't have much tension. If the character doesn't care about the outcome, the reader won't either. For example, in *Just for Show*, the first turning point is when the two main characters sign a contract to enter a fake relationship. The protagonist, Claire, is committed to convincing an acquisition editor she's in a happy relationship so the publishing house will publish her self-help book on relationships.

- **It needs to be this decision that launches the rest of the story.** Without this decision, there would be no story.

- **It needs to be related to whatever happened in the inciting incident.** Your character's decision needs to be a result of the inciting incident. If it's something completely unrelated, you don't have a plot; you have a series of unconnected episodes.

- **Most of the time, it needs to be a choice.** The commitment to the story goal needs to be the main character's decision. There are a few exceptions, though. In some books, the character is trapped by the setting or the circumstances, for example, if the character is kidnapped or stranded on an island. But most of the time, you want to have a protagonist who is active, not passive, and that means making choices and then acting on them.

- **It needs to happen on the page.** Readers need to witness the main character making the decision and understand the reasons for that choice; it can't happen off-screen.

- **It needs to create the central story question in the readers' minds.** The central story question is always whether the main character will achieve their goal. Will the detective solve the case? Will the potential lovers get their happy ending? Will the protagonist save the world from the villain? Will Frodo destroy the ring and save Middle Earth in *The Lord of the Rings*? Will Michael manage to get his big break as an actor while pretending to be a woman in *Tootsie*? The story question is why readers keep reading until the story's climax, when the question is answered. Once the central story question has been asked, the beginning is over and you're breaking into act 2.

- **It needs to happen by the 25 percent mark of the story.** If it happens any later, the beginning will drag. The first turning point is where we fully find out what the story is about, so don't take too long to get your readers to that point. In most modern books, the first turning point happens anywhere between the 15 percent and the 25 percent mark, often at the end of the third chapter.

PLACEMENT OF THE POINT OF NO RETURN

As I just said, it's important for the first turning point not to occur too late in the story, since that will make readers impatient for the "real" story to finally start.

How soon after the inciting incident the point of no return happens depends on the book, though.

In some novels, the inciting incident and the first turning point happen in the same scene, so close together that they are basically the same event. That usually happens whenever your protagonist is thrust into a situation in which they are forced to take action immediately. For example, if the villain has kidnapped the main character's kids, your protagonist will be immediately committed to rescuing them, with a very short or no debate section.

In other books, there might be several scenes between the inciting incident and the point of no return. Additional events happen to make the situation worse and up the stakes until the main character can no longer ignore the problem.

EXERCISE #15:

- Pick up the three novels you analyzed before. Can you pinpoint the point of no return in these novels? Where in the story does it happen? Does it happen in the same scene as the inciting incident, or are there other events in between that nudge the main character to finally accept the call to adventure? How does the author make the protagonist's commitment to their goal clear? What can you learn from the way these three authors handled the first plot point?

EXERCISE #16:

- Now take a look at your own manuscript. Can you pinpoint the point of no return? How does your point of no return compare to the first turning points in the three novels you analyzed? Is there anything you learned from analyzing the other books that you could use to improve your first turning point?
- If you are still planning your story, think about how you will lock your protagonist into the story and make sure there's no way back. What will get them to make that kind of decision? How can you show the decision-making process?

EXERCISE #17:

- Use the must-do's above as a checklist. Does your first turning point meet all of these criteria? For example, is it clear what the character's goal is and that they are committed to that goal? Did you make sure your main character can't back out without negative consequences? Does the point of no return happen by the 25 percent mark, or do you have to tighten the beginning to make the point of no return happen sooner?

PART III—
The do's of writing a great beginning

Part II of this guide hopefully gave you a good idea of the different parts and milestones your opening needs to include. You probably also picked the best place to start your story, either with the inciting incident or, backing up slightly, with a short ordinary world section.

In part III, we'll build on the *where* and take a closer look at the *how*. I'll reveal the tasks that each story opening must accomplish and tell you how to achieve each of them. I'll also teach you how to write a compelling first line and how to hook your readers from page one.

9. The ten tasks every opening needs to accomplish — How to write a kickass beginning

Story beginnings need to accomplish a lot of different things. You don't necessarily have to accomplish all these tasks in the first sentence or even on the first page, but you should achieve them all as soon as possible within the first scene.

ANSWERING READER QUESTIONS

Your opening scene needs to answer the questions that readers have whenever they start a new book so they can settle into the story and enjoy the ride. Typically, the questions readers will approach a book with are:

1. **What kind of story is this?** Is it a science fiction novel, a contemporary romance, or a cozy mystery? Is it a light-hearted read or a dramatic one?
2. **Whose story is this?** Who is the character that readers are supposed to root for?
3. **Who is telling this story?** Who is the narrator? In whose point of view are we?
4. **Why should readers care about the main character?** What about the protagonist and their situation will readers identify and empathize with?
5. **When and where does the story take place?** Is it set in present-day New York, in Paris in 1945, or on a faraway planet 300 years in the future?
6. **What's the story about?** What's the theme of the story? What's the protagonist's goal in the story, and what's the main conflict—the

obstacle that keeps them from obtaining it? What's the protagonist's character arc—the inner journey the character will have to take to overcome their fears and reach their goal in the end?

7. **Why should they keep reading?** Is there something interesting happening on the page, or is there a promise of something interesting to come, for example, a puzzle for mystery readers to solve or a witty first meeting between the characters in a romance? Does the beginning raise questions readers want to have answered?

THE TEN TASKS OF EVERY OPENING

Derived from these reader questions are the ten essential tasks that every beginning needs to accomplish. I'll give you a quick overview of those tasks here, and you can then use it as a checklist to make sure your opening chapter meets all these tasks and answers all the readers' questions.

Your opening should:

1. Hook readers and keep their attention
2. Introduce your main characters
3. Start with action
4. Set the tone and other expectations for the book
5. Establish the time and place
6. Establish the point of view
7. Introduce the character's goal and the stakes involved
8. Initiate the story's conflict
9. Set up the protagonist's character arc
10. Foreshadow the end of the story

I'll explain each task in more detail in the following chapters, so don't worry if you don't yet fully understand how to achieve each task. By the end of this book, you definitely will.

EXERCISE #18:

• Look at each of the three novels you picked to analyze again. Read the first page of each book, and try to answer the seven questions that readers approach a story with. How many of them can you answer at the end of page 1? How many can you answer at the end of the first scene? How many at the end of chapter 1? How long does each novel take to answer all of the questions?

EXERCISE #19:

• Now do the same for your own manuscript. How long does it take you to answer all seven questions? Make sure you use only what's on the page, not just in your head, to answer the questions. Are there any questions you need to answer sooner? How could you accomplish that? Do the three novels you've analyzed give you an idea?

• If you are still in the planning stages of your story, write down the answers to each of the seven questions and think about ways to reveal the answers in the story.

10. Task #1 —
How to hook your readers

We've talked about how important it is to hook your readers, as well as agents and editors, right away, or they'll lose interest and move on to another book.

But what exactly does "hooking" your readers mean, and how do you accomplish it?

WHAT IS A HOOK?

A hook is something—anything—that catches readers' attention and makes them want to read more to find out what's going on and what will happen next.

It can be:
- a puzzle or mystery
- a dangerous or unusual situation
- an unexpected event
- a witty or intriguing line of dialogue
- a clever twist
- a fascinating description
- an interesting character
- a character's unique voice
- a strong emotion
- a sense that something dangerous or interesting will be happening in the future (foreshadowing)
- a jarring element that makes readers pause—and then read on to figure out what's going on

This isn't an exhaustive list. I'm sure there are other elements that would work as a hook too. Basically, a hook is anything that makes readers curious to find out more.

HOW TO HOOK READERS

How exactly do the elements I mentioned above hook readers? As you might have noticed, they all have one thing in common: they raise a question in readers' minds.

Humans are inherently curious. Once a question is formed in our minds, we want to find out the answer, so we continue reading.

Here's the opening line of *The Martian* by Andy Weir as an example:

```
I'm pretty much fucked.
```

Not only does this first line present us with a strong voice, it also immediately raises a question in our minds: Why is this character fucked? What happened? And will he find a way to get out of whatever trouble he's in?

WHEN TO HOOK READERS

How soon do you need to hook readers? As I mentioned before, readers nowadays have short attention spans. The sooner you catch their attention, the better. If your first paragraph fails to do that, they might put the book down and never pick it up again.

So the best place for your hook is in the very first sentence. If you can create an interesting question in readers' minds with your opening line, you'll have them hooked.

But sometimes, you need the first sentence as a setup for the hook you present in the second sentence. For example, look at the opening of *The Lovely Bones* by Alice Sebold:

```
My name was Salmon, like the fish; first name,
Susie. I was fourteen when I was murdered on
December 6, 1973.
```

While the first sentence promises an interesting voice, it doesn't raise a question. The second sentence certainly does, though! Who murdered Susie and why? And how can a dead girl tell us her story?

So the hook doesn't necessarily have to be in your very first sentence. Just make sure it occurs as early as possible. I would advise you to include a hook in your first paragraph.

MUST-DO'S OF AN OPENING HOOK

To effectively capture the reader's interest, a hook has to:

- **Make readers ask at least one specific question** that is relevant to the story.

- **Signal curiosity, not confusion.** The question raised by the hook can't be "huh?" or "who's talking?" or "where the heck is this scene taking place?" You want your question to reflect the reader's curiosity; you don't want it to be a sign that your reader is confused or frustrated.

- **Be genre-specific.** Readers of certain genres will expect to be hooked by certain elements. Make sure your hook fits your target audience. For example, readers of mystery novels would be hooked by an opening line such as the one in *What Came Before He Shot Her* by Elizabeth George:

```
Joel Campbell, eleven years old at the time,
began his descent towards murder with a bus
ride.
```

However, you wouldn't expect a first line like this in a romance or a fantasy novel.

- **Fit the rest of your story.** Your first line sets the tone for the rest of your book. If you start the book with a grisly murder, a sense of danger, or a dramatic situation just to draw the reader in, and then the rest of the story turns out to be a romantic comedy, readers will feel cheated.

- **Be tightly written.** Most of the time, first lines and first paragraphs shouldn't go on for too long. A clear, concise, relatively simple opening paragraph will often work best. Polish your first paragraph, and make sure that every word is necessary and moves the story forward in some way.

EXAMPLES OF BAD FIRST LINES

Let's look at a few examples of unexciting first lines:

```
Tina paid the taxi driver and stepped out of
the cab.
```

Questions raised: none. There's no emotion and no interesting description either. Let's see if we can revise this sentence a little.

Revised version:

```
Tina  stepped  out  of  the  cab,  clutched  her
purse,  and  peeked  through  the  wrought-iron
gates before her.
```

Questions raised: What's on the other side of the gates, and why is it obviously making her nervous?

Here's a second example of a not very gripping opening line:

```
Tina  walked  to  her  car  at  the  back  of  the
parking lot.
```

Again, this sentence doesn't raise any interesting questions.

Revised version:

```
Tina hurried to her car at the back of the dark
parking lot.
```

I changed just one word and added another, but it might make readers wonder why she's hurrying. Is she being followed? Is she scared? Adding the word *dark* establishes the time of day, which helps to evoke an image in readers' minds. The back of a parking lot at night might even create a sense of danger.

EXAMPLES OF GOOD FIRST LINES

Here are a few examples from novels with first lines that raise questions and make me want to read on. Read them and see if you agree.

"Where's Papa going with that axe?" said Fern to her mother as they were setting the table for breakfast.
Charlotte's Web by E.B. White

The apocalypse arrived when Maddie Grey had shampoo in her eyes.
The Brutal Truth by Lee Winter

I write this sitting in the kitchen sink.
I Capture the Castle by Dodie Smith

They shoot the white girl first.
Paradise by Toni Morrison

At approximately seven o'clock on the evening of her twenty-eighth birthday, during an otherwise uneventful Friday night at the office, Dana Watts was confronted by the most perfect pair of naked female breasts she had ever seen.
Thirteen Hours by Meghan O'Brien

The first time I came to Deadwood, I got shot in the ass.
Nearly Departed in Deadwood by Ann Charles

On the second Thursday of the month, Mrs. Dombrowski
brings her dead husband to our therapy group.
The Storyteller by Jodi Picoult

One hot August Thursday afternoon, Maddie Farraday
reached under the front seat of her husband's Cadillac
and pulled out a pair of black lace underpants. They
weren't hers.
Tell Me Lies by Jennifer Crusie

When the phone rang, Parker was in the garage,
killing a man.
Firebreak by Richard Stark

"Fired? What do you mean, you've been fired?"
The Ordinary Princess by Liz Fielding

HOW TO KEEP READERS HOOKED

Okay, now that you have your readers hooked with a great first line,
how do you keep their attention?

The answer is simple: use more hooks. As your opening scene continues,
you will answer some of the questions you raised in readers' minds in
the first paragraph, but not before you create another one, which will
keep readers reading. You'll sprinkle questions throughout your opening
chapter—and the rest of the story—and readers will follow them like a
trail of breadcrumbs.

But if all you do is make readers ask questions while not providing any
answers, readers will grow tired of it before too long. They will start to

think you'll never answer their questions. That's why you need to achieve a good balance in your opening chapter. Answer enough questions not to frustrate or confuse readers, but leave some unanswered and raise new ones so readers will keep turning the pages.

Here's the opening paragraph from *The Hunger Games* by Suzanne Collins as an example:

> When I wake up, the other side of the bed is cold. My fingers stretch out, seeking Prim's warmth but finding only the rough canvas cover of the mattress. She must have had bad dreams and climbed in with our mother. Of course, she did. This is the day of the reaping.

The first sentence raises a question or two: Who's missing and why? Sentence two and three answer those questions, but sentence four immediately sparks another: Why does the protagonist think it's to be expected for Prim to have had a nightmare? The next sentence answers that question and raises the most interesting one so far: What on earth is the reaping, and why is it causing Prim such distress?

See how this string of questions raised and answered works? Before we know it, we have turned the first page to find out. It's not always necessary to answer the questions you create this fast. For example, it takes several more pages until we find out what exactly the reaping is in *The Hunger Games*. By the time we find out, we'll continue reading because we want to find out whose name will be drawn.

END-OF-SCENE & END-OF-CHAPTER HOOKS

So now you have readers hooked with a captivating opening paragraph and are keeping them reading with more hooks throughout your first scene. But what happens when readers reach the end of your opening scene or opening chapter?

Scene and chapter endings are a natural place for readers to put the book down and go to sleep. Your job as an author is not to let them do that. You want them to read "just one more chapter"…and then another, even though it's three a.m. and they have to go to work the next morning.

How do you get them to do that? You probably guessed it: with the help of another hook. At the end of a chapter, that hook is often called a *cliffhanger*.

That term is considered to have originated from serialized fiction that ended with the main character being left dangling off a cliff so readers had to buy the next magazine to find out if the protagonist will survive. But a cliffhanger doesn't always have to mean that your protagonist must be placed in mortal danger at the end of a chapter. Hooking readers at the end of a scene or chapter is accomplished the same way as with the hooks you put in at the beginning or the middle of your scene: by raising questions in the readers' mind. Only this time, you delay the answer until the next scene or chapter so readers will have to keep turning the page to find out.

EXAMPLES FOR END-OF-SCENE & END-OF-CHAPTER HOOKS

Here are a few options for things you could use to create a hook at the end of a scene or chapter.

- **Something unexpected happens.** For example, this is the end of the first chapter of *The Hunger Games* by Suzanne Collins:

  > Effie Trinket crosses back to the podium, smoothes the slip of paper, and reads out the name in a clear voice. And it's not me.
  >
  > It's Primrose Everdeen.

- **Your protagonist makes a decision,** and the reader will have to read on to see how it's going to pan out.

- **A new character arrives.** Here's an example from *The Goldfinch* by Donna Tartt:

  > Standing on the doormat were two people I had never seen in my life: a chubby Korean woman with a short, spiky haircut, a Hispanic guy in shirt and tie who looked a lot like Luis on Sesame Street. There was nothing at all threatening about them, quite the contrary; they were reassuringly dumpy and middle-aged, dressed like a pair of substitute school teachers, but though they both had kindly expressions on their faces, I understood the

instant I saw them that my life, as I knew it, was over.

- **Your protagonist makes a discovery or has a new revelation,** making readers wonder what the character will do with that new piece of information. For example, at the end of the first chapter of *A Trouble of Fools* by Linda Barnes, the main character—a private investigator—discovers that her supposedly poor client isn't so poor after all.

  > I waited for her to pull out a checkbook, but she took a fat leather change purse out of her handbag. She crowded it behind her purse, trying to block my view.
  >
  > By sitting up tall, I had a perfectly clear view of a huge wad of bills. She peeled off ten hundreds, squared the edges neatly, and placed them on the cookie plate.
  >
  > So, don't get me wrong. I'm not saying I didn't think something was fishy from the start.

- **Remind readers of the stakes.** Here's an example:

  > "You'd better hope you're right. If your calculation is off by even a second, we're all going to die."

- **End the scene or chapter with the character encountering a new obstacle** that stands in the way of achieving their goal. Readers will wonder how they are going to overcome that obstacle, so they'll read on to find out.

- **A new situation arises,** and the outcome isn't obvious. For example, in a thriller, you could end the first chapter with the police arriving, making readers wonder how the hostage takers are going to react. Will they now panic and shoot the hostages?

- **Give readers a hint of future trouble (foreshadowing).** Here's an example:

> Sarah kept her gun trained on Smith until he disappeared around the corner. She had a feeling she hadn't seen the last of him.

- Foreshadowing works not just for danger but also for **making readers expect a future scene that will be fun to read**. Here's an example from my fake-relationship romance *The Roommate Arrangement*:

> Now Steph just needed to find a person willing to go along with her plan. Craigslist probably wasn't the right place for that. She chuckled as she imagined the ad. *Wanted: roommate to share two-bedroom apartment. Centrally located, comes with a parking spot, on-site laundry, and a fake relationship.*

> When they crossed the state line into Nevada, she was still amusing herself imagining the kind of person who would answer an ad like that. She couldn't wait to meet him—or her.

As you can see, all of these scene or chapter endings have one thing in common: they leave readers with unanswered questions. It might sound strange, but don't finish every chapter with a resolution of a situation. If everything is neatly wrapped up, that doesn't give readers a reason to continue reading. Instead, end the chapter with a *beginning*—something new happening.

DOES EVERY CHAPTER NEED A CLIFFHANGER?

Not every scene or chapter has to end with a cliffhanger. If you use them too often, they lose their impact. As long as readers still have at least one unanswered question in their minds that encourages them to keep reading, it's okay not to end every chapter with a big surprise.

Definitely put some extra work into the end of the first scene, the first chapter, and the first act, though. These are the danger areas where readers could be tempted to put your book down, so make sure they all end with a pressing question that urges readers to turn the page.

EXERCISE #20:

- Surprise! You thought we were going to look at the same three books again, didn't you? No, not this time. It's time to pick some new ones. Go to your bookshelf or get your reading device and pick three different novels in your chosen genre. If you don't want to use novels you already know, go to a library or an online retailer's website and look at samples from five best-selling novels in your genre. Read the first paragraph on the first page only. Does it include a hook? What questions did the author raise in your mind? If the novel doesn't make you want to keep reading, can you tell why? What can you learn from the novels that grabbed your attention—and from the ones that didn't?

EXERCISE #21:

- Now look at your own manuscript. Do you have a hook? Where in the story did you find the first thing that captured your attention and made you ask a question? If it wasn't in the first paragraph, can you rearrange your opening to get the hook into the first paragraph, maybe even the first sentence? Or can you revise your opening in another way to make sure you have a hook in the first paragraph? Can you maybe include an element similar to the ones you found in the novels you analyzed in the previous exercise?
- If you are still planning your book, what kind of hook will you put into your opening paragraph? Feel free to skip the exercises in this chapter, though, and work on your first line and your hooks once you have finished the first draft. As I said earlier, the first line of the book doesn't need to be the first line you write. Sometimes it makes sense not to worry about the opening paragraph until you know how the story will end. Just make sure you come back to do these exercises during the revision phase.

EXERCISE #22:

- Pick up the three novels you analyzed in exercise #20. This time, look at the ending of chapter one for each of them. How did each author end their first chapter? Did they have a hook that made you want to keep reading? Did you feel you could learn anything from how they ended their opening chapters?

EXERCISE #23:

- Read your opening chapter and write down all the questions you raise in the readers' minds. Are you answering all of them in the first chapter? If you feel you are, you might want to go back and leave at least one of them unanswered. Make sure your first chapter ends on a hook that will keep readers turning the page.
- If you are still planning your book, where would be a good place to end the first chapter? What hook could get readers to turn the page and start reading chapter 2?

11. Task #2 —
How to introduce your main characters

One of the most important things your beginning needs to do is to introduce your main characters and let readers know whose story they are going to read. For most readers, what keeps them reading (and re-reading) a book is not the plot but the characters. Without at least one character they can empathize with, they won't care about the story either. Think about it for a minute. Aren't you the same as a reader? Isn't it the characters that get you invested in a story?

WHEN TO INTRODUCE YOUR PROTAGONIST

To avoid confusing your readers, you need to let them know right away who your main character is. Don't make them care for a character only to reveal a few pages later that they're only a side character who won't show up again or who might even get killed off.

How can you let readers know who the protagonist is without actually saying so? By starting the story with the main character and focusing on them in the first scene. Readers are a bit like newly hatched chicks. They will bond with the very first character they meet and assume this is the protagonist. If the most prominent character in your opening scene isn't your protagonist, you might want to rewrite your beginning. Ideally, readers should meet your protagonist in the very first sentence or as close to it as possible. Keep the opening scene focused on your main character, so readers will understand that this is the person they are supposed to care about.

HOW TO INTRODUCE YOUR PROTAGONIST

Okay, now that you know what character to introduce first, let's focus on how to introduce them. Here are the most important tips:

- Don't just start with the protagonist; **start with them doing something interesting**. Avoid introducing your main character in a static—and boring—situation. Don't open the book with the protagonist reflecting on their life or current situation while they're not really doing anything of interest. Blocks of introspection make for a passive character and a very slow opening. I'll discuss that problem in more depth later. For now, just know that you need to avoid having your character sitting and thinking in the first chapter. Give them something more interesting to do than just washing the dishes or brushing their teeth. Have your character deal with a problem, encounter a conflict, or have an interesting conversation.

- **Ideally, open with the protagonist in a characteristic moment.** Have them do something that reveals important personality traits. But don't give readers a list of personality traits in the first scene. Instead, focus on showing readers the character's defining trait— what makes them *them*. For example, my historical romance novel *Shaken to the Core* opens with the main character, Giuliana, worrying about her brother. That shows us she's loyal and used to taking care of her family. Try to show readers the essence of your protagonist's personality as early as possible. If your character's dominant trait is that they're witty and snarky, have them banter with someone in the opening scene.

- **Show your character's personality; don't explain it to us.** While you are letting your readers know about your protagonist's dominant traits, remember to follow the cardinal writing rule: show, don't tell. Here's an example from my novel *Just for Show*:

> Telling: `Claire was overly organized and neat.`
> Showing: `Claire wrung out the wet rag Lana had left in the sink, folded it, and hung it over the faucet.`

Readers want to make up their own minds about a character's personality by watching what they are doing and drawing their own conclusions instead of having you interpret the character's actions for them. Make sure you reveal your character's personality traits through their actions, their dialogue, their thoughts, and their body language, not by simply stating them.

- **Don't reveal everything you know about your main character in the first chapter.** I know it can be tempting, especially if you have created detailed character profiles and know everything about your characters, down to their first crush and favorite ice cream flavors. But readers don't need to know all of that in the first chapter. Let readers get to know your characters the same way we get to know people in real life: slowly and bit by bit. You'll find more advice on how to do that in chapter 21.

- **Establish the character's strength or competence.** In the first scene, show readers something your protagonist does well. That skill will often become important later in the book. For example, if your character is going to win a fight against three opponents later on, show us the protagonist's martial arts medals in the opening scene.

- **Give readers a sense of the protagonist's fears, flaws, or internal issues.** Perfect characters are unrealistic and boring since they have no room to grow. To make your protagonist three-dimensional, they can't have only strengths and positive traits. They need a weakness, fear, or flaw too. During the course of the novel, they will usually overcome that flaw. The flaw they start out with is often the flip side of their strength or dominant personality trait. For example, Marlin in *Finding Nemo* is a caring father, but he's also overprotective and fearful. If your character is ambitious (strength), they might also be a workaholic (flaw). If they are independent, they might have difficulties trusting or relying on others. Their fear or flaw might stem from unhealed psychological wounds from their past. It doesn't necessarily have to be a traumatic event, just something that hurt your character enough to shape who they are today. For example, in my novel *The Roommate Arrangement,* Rae has been made fun of because of her hippie parents and their alternative lifestyle. As a result, she fears being ridiculed in public and will go to great lengths to avoid public embarrassment as an adult.

- **Give readers some insight into the character's emotions.** Readers read novels for the emotional experience, so let them in on what your character is feeling in the opening scene. Again, make sure you *show* those emotions instead of *telling* readers about them. Here's an example that demonstrates the difference:

> Telling emotions: `She was relieved.`
> Showing emotions: *Oh, thank God!* `She pressed her hand to her chest.`

If you want to learn more about how to show your characters' emotions, check out my writers' guide *Show, Don't Tell.*

Ideally, you should accomplish all of these things in the opening scene. At times, that won't be possible, but try to establish as many of these points in the first scene as you can and then check off the rest within the first chapter.

HOW TO GET READERS TO CARE ABOUT YOUR MAIN CHARACTER

Your book's opening shouldn't just introduce your main characters; it should also make readers care about them. It's that emotional bond that will keep readers turning the pages because they want to find out whether the protagonist is going to make it through all the obstacles you've thrown at them.

That doesn't mean that readers need to love everything about a character right away, but there has to be something readers can identify with from the start.

So how do you get readers to care? Here are some tips:

- **Make your main characters relatable.** Even if they are billionaires, rock stars, werewolves, or witches, there needs to be something about them that readers can relate to.

- **Give your main character at least one admirable trait.** For example, show that your protagonist has a great sense of humor or does something kind or brave. That's where the title of Blake Snyder's screenwriting book *Save the Cat* comes from. In his book, he suggests having the main character do something caring or brave—such as risking their own life to save a cat—to make them likable.

- **Put your main characters in a situation that will make readers feel sympathetic with them.** Usually, we feel sorry for a person who has some kind of undeserved misfortune or who experiences embarrassment, rejection, or mistreatment. For example, the first scene of my romance novel *Just for Show* starts with Claire's fiancée breaking up with her.

- **Make your main characters experience an emotion readers can empathize with.** Even if readers have never been in the exact same situation as the main character, it needs to arouse a universal emotion that readers are familiar with, for example, grief or embarrassment.

- **Make sure your readers can understand your main character's motivation.** Even if they can't identify with the protagonist's goal, they need to be able to relate to the main character's reason for trying to achieve that goal. For example, in my paranormal romance *Second Nature*, my main character Griffin is a shape-shifter who's sent out to kill a human—not a goal that makes her very likable. But the motivation behind it is one that will hopefully resonate with readers: Griffin wants to protect the secret existence of her species, which is on the brink of extinction. Wanting to protect the people you love is something my readers should be able to identify with.

You don't have to accomplish all of these things in the first scene—establishing the character's motivation might have to wait until later, for example—but make sure your opening scene does at least some of these things so readers can start bonding with the protagonist right away.

WHAT OTHER CHARACTERS TO INTRODUCE IN THE BEGINNING

Of course, it's not enough to have just your protagonist in the opening chapters of your book. Here are some thoughts on other characters you will have to introduce during the first act.

- **Love interest.** If you are writing a romance or have a romantic subplot in your novel, you need to introduce the love interest early on. Actually, I'd argue that most romance novels have two main characters (or more than two if you're writing about a polyamorous relationship). Sometimes, we'll spend more time in one character's point of view, usually the character who has more profound fears and flaws to overcome before they can let themselves fall in love. In that case, that character might be more of a protagonist than the other and will get introduced first. But no matter what, you need to introduce all the main characters of a romance as soon as possible. The future lovers should usually meet in the first chapter—or in chapter two or three at the latest.

- **Antagonist.** Every story needs an antagonist, even if you're not writing a thriller or a mystery. An antagonist doesn't necessarily have to be a serial killer or an evil villain out to destroy the world. The antagonist is simply the person who blocks the protagonist from reaching their goal. Even if you have a villain, make them a three-dimensional person with strengths, weaknesses, and a good reason for doing whatever they are doing. Make sure the antagonist is a worthy opponent who can't be outsmarted too easily. Introduce your antagonist in the first act. Even if we don't see them on the page in the opening chapters, you need to at least foreshadow your antagonist. J.K. Rowling did it that way in her *Harry Potter* series. We don't meet Voldemort in the first act of book 1, but we find out he killed Harry's parents.

- **Other major characters.** The first act is also the place to introduce other *major* characters. Notice the emphasis on *major*. If there are any other characters who will turn out to be important to the plot, you might want to introduce them in the first act. But be careful not to introduce too many characters in the opening chapter. Readers may not be able to keep them all apart and might end up confused. In particular, try to keep minor characters out of the opening scene or, if you need them, make it clear that they are only minor characters. How do you do that? Don't spend any time on them. If you introduce a character by name and describe them, readers will automatically assume that person is important. So, for example, if your book starts with your protagonist getting out of a cab, refer to the taxi driver as "the taxi driver" without giving them a name or describing them in detail.

EXERCISE #24:

- Pick three novels in your genre that include your favorite characters. Read the first chapter of each. How many characters are introduced in the first scene? How many in the first chapter? When do we meet the protagonist? How is the main character introduced? What do we learn about them in the first chapter? What makes the protagonist likable? Is there anything you can learn from how these authors introduce their characters?

EXERCISE #25:

- Now take a look at your own manuscript. When do we meet your protagonist? Do you need to introduce them sooner? Have you managed to make your protagonist likable? How many characters have you introduced in the first scene? How many in the first chapter? Are there too many characters, especially too many minor characters? Is it clear that they are minor characters? Would it be better to cut some of them out? Try it and see if the scene still works.
- If you are still in the planning stages, when are you intending to introduce your main character? Will we meet them on page one? How many characters will you introduce in your opening scene? How many will readers meet in the first chapter?

EXERCISE #26:

- What is your main character's dominant trait? If you had to describe them in one word, what would that word be?
- What's your main character's fear or flaw?
- Did you reveal that dominant trait and give readers a sense of the flaw or fear in the opening scene? Did you make sure readers will find something to like about your main character? If you are still planning your novel, think about how you could reveal your protagonist's dominant trait, a likable characteristic, and the fear or flaw in the opening scene.

EXERCISE #27:

- Read your first scene. Now make a list of things we learn about your main character(s) in that first scene. Include just things that you actually put into the first scene, not things that you as the author know about the character(s).

- Have you *shown* us these things or *told* us about them? If you have told us, how could you show us instead?

- If you are still planning your novel, make a list of things you want readers to find out about your main character in the first scene. Use the "how to introduce your protagonist" list above as a guideline. Think about how to *show* readers your character's defining trait, likable characteristics, strengths, and flaws.

12. Task #3 —
How to start in medias res

Some editors and writing coaches tell authors to "open with action," but I think that's both great and really bad advice, depending on the book and its genre and on your interpretation of what that suggestion means.

DON'T (NECESSARILY) OPEN WITH BULLETS FLYING

If you take that advice to mean you should open your book with an action scene—a bomb going off, a gun fight, a high-speed car chase—that probably won't work for most books. The problem is that readers haven't had time to bond with the characters yet, so they don't care if they survive this dangerous situation. They might not even know yet who the main character is or who they should be rooting for. That's why it's often a good idea to back up a little and give readers at least a paragraph or two to establish that bond during a short ordinary world section, as described in chapter 5, before putting your character in danger.

So if "start with action" doesn't mean "start with an action scene," what does it really mean?

START IN THE MIDDLE OF THINGS

It means start *in medias res*, which is Latin for "in the middle of things." A lot of writers begin their book with background information on the character or the story world or with an explanation of how the character got into the situation. But fiction readers read to be entertained, not lectured. They want to experience what's happening in the present before they learn about the past.

What "starting with action" really means is to open with an interesting situation already in progress or a character pursuing a goal. Cut out all the information and instead show readers the actions and the dialogue. Throw the reader headlong into the story, have something interesting happen right away, and fill in the explanations in bits and pieces later. Don't wait too long for the inciting incident to take place, and if you delay it for a bit, make sure you have enough interesting things happening on the page to keep readers captivated until the big event throws your characters' lives out of balance.

As I mentioned before, a common mistake that makes editors and readers stop reading is the sitting-and-thinking scenario, when the story opens with the character reflecting on their life. Static characters are boring. Instead, give your characters something interesting to do. Show them pursuing a goal, even if it's not yet the goal they'll try to achieve throughout the rest of the book.

Here's an example from the first page of *Survival Instincts* by May Dawney, a dystopian novel:

> The first sign that New York City would be special was the zebra. It pushed through the shrubbery and onto the sun-flooded interstate no more than thirty feet from Lynn. Its hooves clicked on the cracked asphalt as it weaved its way leisurely through the thick throng of rusted car skeletons.

Lynn stopped.

Skeever, at her heels, did too.

At least for now, the zebra didn't notice them. It plucked at a tuft of grass with nimble lips.

Lynn blinked consciously, wondering if the animal would go away if she did. It didn't. If this animal was what she thought it was, she was staring at an Old-World relic. The striped horses had been kept in carefully constructed habitats in the hearts of cities. Lynn realized she should probably have felt awed by the experience, but her only thought was *dinner*. She quietly reached down to her belt and undid the leather strap that held her tomahawk in place.

While we get some information about the setting, the author doesn't stop the action to explain what has happened to this world. Instead, we follow the main character as she goes about her goal—hunting for dinner.

We'll revisit this topic in more detail in part IV, where I'll tell you more about how to avoid information dumps and handle backstory and descriptions.

EXERCISE #28:

- Pick any three novels in your genre. If you are tired of the ones you have already analyzed for previous exercises, choose three new books. Take a look at the first page. Did the authors start in the middle of things? What are the main characters doing on page 1? Are they pursuing any goals?

EXERCISE #29:

- Look at the opening page of your own novel again. Are you showing your character in action? Imagine your book is being filmed as a movie. What would we be seeing the actors do on screen? Is there enough happening, or is your beginning too static?

13. Task #4 —
How to set the tone and other expectations

The opening of your story makes a promise to readers about what kind of book it is going to be. Your beginning sets up expectations about the book's genre, tone, mood, theme, and pacing. Is it going to be a funny romantic comedy, an action-packed thriller, a suspenseful mystery, or a witty young adult novel?

To avoid breaking that promise and disappointing readers, make sure your opening is consistent with the rest of the book.

PROMISES TO KEEP

Here are a few of the promises your beginning is making. Keep an eye on each of them to make sure you're not promising one thing and delivering another.

- **Your book's genre.** The opening scene should clearly indicate the genre and subgenre, which will already be revealed by the book's title, cover, and blurb. In a romance novel, it's not always possible to include typical "romance" elements in the first scene if the main characters haven't met yet, but you should at least not use any elements that indicate other genres. For example, don't open your sweet romance novel with a gritty murder scene. If the opening of your urban fantasy reads as if it's a contemporary romance, but then you suddenly throw in witches or vampires on page 25, readers will feel betrayed. If you are writing urban fantasy taking place in a setting that looks like our normal world, find a way to indicate on page 1 that this is, in fact, a different world. Here's an example—the opening paragraph of *1984* by George Orwell.

> It was a bright cold day in April, and the clocks were striking thirteen. Winston Smith, his chin nuzzled into his breast in an effort to escape the vile wind, slipped quickly through the glass doors of Victory Mansions, though not quickly enough to prevent a swirl of gritty dust from entering along with him.

At first glance, the novel could be set in England, but bright April days usually aren't that cold, and clocks certainly don't strike thirteen in our world. (Even in countries that use the 24-hour system, analog clocks only mark twelve hours, so at 1 p.m. or 13:00, the clocks should only strike once, not thirteen times).

- **Your book's tone.** Tone refers to the attitude of a story's narrator. Is the book upbeat or pessimistic, serious or humorous, warm or uncaring, hopeful or defeated, sad or joyful? The tone on the first page should be consistent with the tone in the rest of the book. If you are writing a funny, light-hearted book, make sure the opening is funny and light-hearted too. Here's an example from the opening of *Bridget Jones's Diary* by Helen Fielding:

> Noon. London: my flat. Ugh. The last thing on earth I feel physically, emotionally or mentally equipped to do is drive to Una and Geoffrey Alconbury's New Year's Day Turkey Curry Buffet in Grafton Underwood. Geoffrey and Una Alconbury are my parents' best friends

> and, as Uncle Geoffrey never tires of reminding
> me, have known me since I was running round the
> lawn with no clothes on. My mother rang up at
> 8:30 in the morning last August Bank Holiday
> and forced me to promise to go. She approached
> it via a cunningly circuitous route.

I'd say the tone is personal—as is to be expected from a diary—humorous, and self-deprecating.

- **Your book's pace.** If you open your book with a high-speed car chase, readers will expect a fast-paced thriller, not a character-driven coming-of-age story full of lyrical descriptions. That's why it's important not to rely on gimmicky first lines to hook your readers. They might succeed in capturing the attention of your readers, but if the rest of the story can't keep up, you'll quickly lose them.

EXERCISE #30:

• Pick three novels in your genre that you know well. Read page 1. What promises does the first page make? Does the rest of the book keep those promises? Is the tone on page 1 indicative of the tone in the rest of the book?

EXERCISE #31:

• Now look at page 1 of your own manuscript. What promises are you making to your readers? Are you keeping those promises in the rest of the book? For example, does the opening indicate the book's genre? Does the tone of your opening continue for the duration of the story? Is the pacing consistent throughout the rest of the book? If the answer to any of these three questions is no, how can you revise your beginning in a way that sets the right expectations?

14. Task #5 —
How to establish the time and place

Two of the questions that readers approach each story with are: Where are we? When is this story taking place? If you have ever been lost, you know how unsettling and disorienting it can be, so don't do that to your readers. Give them a sense of where and when the story is taking place as quickly as you can.

Are we in London? A small town in rural Iowa? A school for wizards? A planet far, far away? Is the story set in the present, the past, or the future? Is it winter, spring, fall, or summer; morning, afternoon, or the middle of the night?

HOW TO ANCHOR READERS IN THE SETTING

Here are a few important tips to help you establish the time and place of your story.

- **Less is more.** Give readers enough details to help them get oriented in the setting, but don't go overboard and overwhelm readers with too much information about your story world. I'll give you more advice on how to avoid slow beginnings and handle descriptions in chapter 21 of this guide.

- **Use multiple senses.** Don't go overboard and use all five senses any time you describe a setting, but try to include at least one sense other than sight in your descriptions. Sound, smell, taste, and touch can be used to make a setting come alive to readers. Here's an example from the opening paragraph of *The Last Dragon Princess* by Cynthia Payne:

> For hours now, the only sounds besides the music had been the constant *swish-swish-swish* of the painter's brush.

• **Make sure your description is not violating the character's point of view.** Describe only what your POV character would notice and stop to think about given their background, personality, and situation. Different people notice different things. An interior designer would notice the colors and the arrangement of furniture in a room, while a firefighter would look for the exits. Does your character really have a good reason to notice and think about the setting right now? For example, if the character is in a familiar place, they wouldn't pay any attention to the furniture or the color of the curtains. If you want to describe the protagonist's house or place of work, you have to give them a good reason why they'd notice these details. Is something different about their surroundings than usual, therefore making it catch the character's eye?

• **Don't just give us objective descriptions; indicate how your POV character feels about their surroundings.** Remember that your character is not an objective camera that just records everything without emotion. Don't just give readers the facts about the setting, but show subtle indications of what emotions the setting evokes in your character. Here's an example:

Objective description: The smell of disinfectant was prominent.

Subjective description: The hallway reeked of disinfectant.

- **Descriptions of the setting should also reveal something about the point of view character.** What they notice and what words they choose to describe something should tell readers something about the character's personality, mood, and attitude toward the location. Here's the first line from *Uglies* by Scott Westerfeld as an example:

  ```
  The  early  summer  sky  was  the  color  of  cat
  vomit.
  ```

- **Use nouns that are concrete and specific.** For example, instead of saying house, use bungalow or mansion.

- **Use strong, dynamic verbs, not weak, static ones**. Static verbs are any form of "to have" or "to be," among others, while dynamic verbs evoke images in readers' minds and create a sense of motion. For example, *tiptoed* and *ambled* are often better than *walked*.

  Static description: It was cold.
  Dynamic description: The cold air stung Sarah's
  cheeks.

- **Use fresh metaphors and similes that fit the POV character's personality.** Here's an example from *Crave* by J.R. Ward:

  ```
  "This is it," Matthias said as they came up to
  an abandoned village that was the color of the
  caramel on a Friendly's sundae.
  ```

EXERCISE #32:

• Look at the three novels you analyzed in the last chapter again. How did the authors establish the time and place? How much description of the setting did you find in the opening scene? Did you feel that there was too much description at any point in the opening scene, bogging it down? What nouns and verbs did they use to describe the setting? Did they make use of senses other than sight?

EXERCISE #33:

• Now do the same analysis for your own book. Did you establish the time and place as quickly as possible? Is there too much description, slowing the pace? Are you using specific nouns and active verbs? Did you make use of senses other than sight? Did you make sure not to violate point of view by describing something your POV character wouldn't pay attention to? Use the list above to revise your opening scene.

15. Task #6 —
How to establish the point of view

Let me start this chapter with a quick definition to make sure we're on the same page. Point of view (POV) is the perspective from which a story—or at least a section of a story—is told. It's like a lens through which readers view the events.

I go into a lot more detail on POV in my writers' guide *Point of View*, but for the purpose of this book, let me just say that nowadays, most genre fiction novels are written from the point of view of the protagonist, either using first person pronouns (I) or third person pronouns (usually *he* or *she*).

FIRST PERSON OR THIRD PERSON?

One of the choices you are going to have to make before starting your novel is picking your POV. Decide whether you'll write in first-person or third-person POV and whether you'll have one or several POV characters, for example, switching back and forth between your two main characters.

Both types of POV come with their advantages and disadvantages. First-person POV is very intimate and immediate, creating a close connection between character and reader, but a lot of readers dislike first-person. I suspect it's partly because first-person POV is difficult to do well, but it looks deceptively easy. As a result, many writers use it before they have the skills to pull it off and create a strong enough voice for a first-person narrative.

Make sure you are familiar with the do's and don'ts of your chosen point of view.

Your choice of POV might also be influenced by your preferred genre. For example, first-person POV is common in young adult and urban fantasy novels, while third-person POV dominates the romance genre.

ESTABLISHING POV

Just as you should establish the *when* and *where* of the story right away, you also need to establish the *who* as soon as possible, ideally with the very first sentence.

I strongly suggest starting the story in your protagonist's point of view. If you open the book in the viewpoint of a minor character, readers will assume that this is the main character.

One of the biggest mistakes I see novice writers making is opening their story with no clear point of view. They will describe the weather or the location or some other detail of their story world for several paragraphs without mentioning the character we should be experiencing the setting with.

Instead, filter everything you show your readers through the protagonist's senses, revealing only details that the character would notice. Dip into the character's heart and mind to let us know what they're feeling and thinking, but be careful not to bog down the story with blocks of internalization.

Here's an example from the opening of *Trading in Danger* by Elizabeth Moon:

> ```
> Kylara Vatta came to attention in front of the
> Commandant's desk. One sheet of flatcopy lay in
> front of him, the print too small for her to
> read upside down. She had a bad feeling about
> this.
> ```

The author gets us into the main character's point of view in the second sentence by letting us see through Kylara's eyes. The third sentence brings us even closer, revealing her feelings. We don't get a description of the commandant's office or an explanation of what a flatcopy is, since that would violate Kylara's point of view. She has been in the office before, and of course, she knows what a flatcopy is, so she has no reason to think about either in this scene.

Also remember to show the POV character's feelings and thoughts instead of telling readers about them.

> Telling: `John was stunned by her confidence.`
> Showing: `John's gaze followed her as she strode past, head held high. Wow.`

POV SWITCHES

If you choose to tell your story from multiple points of view, there are a few additional things you need to keep in mind:

- **Don't switch POV too soon.** Give readers some time to settle into the story and bond with one character first. Many writers stay in one

POV for the first chapter, then switch at the beginning of the second chapter.

- On the other hand, **don't wait too long before you switch POV for the first time.** Establish that you are using multiple points of view in the first act. If you tell the story from only one POV for the first fifty pages, that sets up the expectation that it's going to be a single-POV story. If you then switch POV, it will confuse your readers.

- **Never switch point of view within a scene.** That would be considered head hopping, and it's highly confusing for readers. Switch POV either at the start of a new chapter or after a visual scene break such as * * * or a blank line.

- **After every POV switch, establish the new POV character right away.** Try to get readers into the new viewpoint character's head in the first sentence of the scene, if possible.

EXERCISE #34:

• Look at three novels in your genre. What point of view do the authors use? First person or third person? Is there a trend or preferred POV in your genre? How do these authors establish POV at the beginning of the book? If they are using multiple POVs, how long do they stay in one viewpoint, and how do they switch to a new POV? Is there anything you can learn from how these authors handle point of view?

EXERCISE #35:

• Now look at your own manuscript. What point of view did you choose and why? Is the POV you chose popular in your genre? Are you opening the book in the POV of your protagonist? Did you establish the POV right away? If you decided to use multiple points of views, did you switch to a different POV too soon or too late?

• If you are still planning your novel, what POV will you use—first or third person, single or multiple POVs? Whose POV will you start with, and how long will you stay in that POV?

16. Task #7 —
How to introduce the protagonist's goal and stakes

As I mentioned in chapter 5, an opening with an active character will draw readers in, while a passive one will be boring. That's why you need to give your protagonist a goal in the opening scene. Let your readers know what the character wants right now.

Here's an example from my historical romance *Shaken to the Core*:

> Today was the day. Nervous energy prickled down Kate's spine as she headed for the morning room. She hoped she would be able to sit still during breakfast. Her mother hated it when she fidgeted. She took her place at the mahogany table, pulled her linen napkin from its silver ring, and spread it across her lap. "Good morning, Mother. Morning, Father."
>
> "Good morning," her father said, glancing up from his newspaper.
>
> With any luck, she would soon provide the photographs for this very newspaper. The thought made her giddy.

We find out what Kate wants right away: to become a newspaper photographer.

OVERALL STORY GOAL VS. GOAL IN THE FIRST SCENE

That immediate goal in the opening scene doesn't necessarily have to be the ultimate goal that your protagonist will try to achieve in the rest of the book. That goal will only be triggered by the inciting incident, and the main character will fully commit to it in the first turning point, so it's not always possible to introduce that overall story goal in the opening scene.

Even if it's not, give your main character something they want to keep things interesting for the reader until you do introduce the character's big story goal. It can be something simple and relatively small. For example, in my historical romance *Hidden Truths*, the main character is trying to make it to the cotton mill where she works on time. How your protagonist goes about achieving their goal will *show* readers a lot about their personality instead of you having to *tell* readers about it.

If you can, tie the smaller goal in the first scene to the overall story goal. Could both goals be motivated by the same need? For example, in the opening scene of my romance novel *Just for Show*, Claire wants to make sure everything is perfect for her engagement party. That's not her story goal, but it shows readers that she's a perfectionist who micromanages everything. Her story goal is introduced later in the book, at the end of chapter 2: convincing the acquisition editor of a nonfiction publishing house that she's in a happy relationship so they'll publish her relationship self-help book. Both the big story goal and the smaller goal in the opening scene are tied together by the same motivation: Claire's need to appear perfect.

ESTABLISH THE STAKES

If the big story goal doesn't matter to the character, it won't matter to readers either. Something needs to be at stake, and that something has to be important to your protagonist. What does your character stand to gain if they achieve their goal? What will be lost if they fail?

The stakes don't always have to be life or death, but whatever is on the line needs to matter to your protagonist.

For example, in my paranormal romance *Second Nature*, the stakes are high. Shape-shifter Griffin is sent out to kill a human to stop her from revealing the shape-shifters' secret existence, which would drive them even closer to extinction.

The stakes in my contemporary romance *Damage Control* are subtler. Actress Grace has to convince the public that she's straight, or her career will suffer.

EXERCISE #36:

- Look at any three novels in your genre. What goals do the characters have in the opening scenes, and how do the authors reveal these goals? At what point in the story is the big story goal revealed? Hint: Look at the inciting incident and the first turning point of the story. What's at stake?

EXERCISE #37:

- Now look at your own manuscript. Did you give the main character a goal in the opening scene? If you didn't, now is the time to revise. What's the protagonist's story goal, and when is it revealed? Did you make it clear what the stakes are?
- If you are in the planning stages, what goal will you give your protagonist in the opening scene? What goal is your character trying to achieve in the rest of the book, and what's at stake if they fail?

17. Task #8 —
How to initiate conflict

A lack of conflict is one of the most common problems I see in the manuscripts I edit. Conflict is the driving force in stories. Without conflict, there is no story. If characters achieved their goals without effort and worry, there would be no tension, no suspense, and no character growth. Imagine Frodo walking up Mount Doom and dropping the ring into the fiery depths of the volcano, destroying it without any previous struggle. *The Lord of the Rings* would have been a very short and boring book if Tolkien had written it that way.

WHAT IS CONFLICT?

Contrary to what some people believe, conflict doesn't mean that your characters have to be at each other's throats the entire time, or that you have to include battle scenes, arguments, and fist fights in your book. Conflict is what happens if your character wants something, but someone or something blocks them from achieving it.

The simple formula is this: conflict = goal + obstacle

Here's an example from a romance novel that—literally—starts with a bang: *Wallbanger* by Alice Clayton.

    "Oh, God."

    Thump.

"Oh, God."

Thump thump.

What the...

"Oh, God, that's so good!"

I scrambled up out of sleep, confused as I looked around the strange room. Boxes on the floor. Pictures propped against the wall.

Instead of opening it with an explanation about Caroline just having moved into a new apartment with a neighbor who likes very enthusiastic, very noisy sex, the author throws us into the situation and lets us experience it right along with the main character. Caroline's goal in this scene is simple: getting a good night's sleep. But her neighbor is making it impossible. That's conflict.

CONFLICT IN YOUR OPENING SCENE

An opening with happy characters and a perfect world in which everything is going right won't be very interesting to your readers. Like every scene, your opening scene needs conflict. It doesn't necessarily have to be the major conflict of the story yet, but there has to be some kind of conflict, as in the example from *Wallbanger* by Alice Clayton. Show your character trying to solve a problem in their ordinary world. It could be a small, subtle problem, for example, the character has to get to work on time (goal), but they're stuck in a traffic jam (obstacle).

Show that something isn't going the way the protagonist wanted or expected. In the previous chapter, we talked about giving your protagonist a goal. To initiate conflict, introduce an obstacle that keeps the character from reaching that goal. Then show readers how your character reacts to conflict—does your character who's stuck in the traffic jam angrily shout at the other drivers and pound the steering wheel? Do they sigh in frustration and keep sipping their vanilla latte? Or do they call their boss and apologize profusely because they are going to be late?

If you don't open with your big story conflict, see if you can hint at it or introduce a smaller conflict that is in some way related to the major conflict. For example, the first Harry Potter book doesn't open with the big conflict between Harry and Voldemort. It opens with Mr. Dursley sensing something unusual is going on—strangely dressed people in town, owls flying by daylight. His goal is to convince everyone that the Dursleys are perfectly normal people, but with the unusual things going on and odd people bringing up his dead brother-in-law and sister-in-law, the Potters, that goal is in jeopardy.

MAJOR CONFLICT

As I said previously, it's not always possible or necessary to introduce the major conflict in the opening scene, but you do need to establish it in act 1. Show what stands in the way of your protagonist achieving their big story goal.

For example, Kate's goal in my historical romance *Shaken to the Core* is to become a newspaper photographer. But it's 1906, and the newspaper editor thinks women aren't suited to that kind of work, and her parents don't want her to have a job because it would narrow her marital prospects.

CONFLICT AND YOUR GENRE

In plot-driven novels such as mysteries, thrillers, or speculative fiction, the main conflict of the story is always the obstacles getting in the way of the protagonist's major external goal. The detective wants to solve the case, but the serial killer is smart and doesn't leave behind enough evidence. Frodo wants to destroy the ring in *The Lord of the Rings*, but Sauron and his minions, along with several other obstacles (swamps, the weather...), stand in the way.

Romance novels most often have several conflicts. First, both main characters usually have an external goal, and those goals will be met with obstacles. For example, Claire's fiancée breaking up with her stands in the way of getting her self-help book published in *Just for Show*. The real goal in a romance novel is always finding love, though, so the central conflict is the romantic conflict—whatever stands in the way of their relationship. Sometimes, the characters' external goals are obstacles for love, for example, when the potential lovers are competing for the same job or one of them is aiming for a promotion that would mean having to move to another city. Most often, the major obstacle will be the characters' own fears and wounds from the past. That's called internal conflict because it stems from inside of the character. I'll talk more about that in the next chapter.

EXERCISE #38:

- Look at the three novels you analyzed in the previous chapter. What goals did you identify in exercise #36? What gets in the way of the characters achieving those goals? What's the conflict in the opening scene? What are the major obstacles standing in the way of the big story goal?

EXERCISE #39:

- Now do the same analysis for your own manuscript. What obstacles stand in the way of the character's goal in the opening scene? What's your major conflict—the obstacles the protagonist has to overcome during the rest of the story? Do you have enough conflict, both in the opening scene and in the rest of the book?
- If you are still planning your book, identify the obstacles getting in the way of the protagonist's goal in the opening scene, and make a list of obstacles blocking the character's path to their major story goal.

18. Task #9 —
How to set up the protagonist's character arc

The characters who fascinate us most are usually dynamic characters—characters who grow and change during the course of a novel. They start out with some kind of flaw, fear, or misguided belief, which they'll have to overcome by the end of the book.

WHAT IS A CHARACTER ARC?

That inner journey is called a character arc. It's the emotional change a character goes through over the course of the story. That change is what will eventually enable them to achieve their goal and get their happy ending.

HOW TO ESTABLISH A CHARACTER ARC

- To create a believable character arc, you have to **establish the need for change and show readers the character's baseline.** Ideally, reveal your protagonist's flaw or fear in the very first scene. For example, Claire's flaw in my romance novel *Just for Show* is her need to appear perfect. Early in the book, she gets herself into quite a predicament when she lies to a colleague about being in a new relationship, because she doesn't want to appear like a heartbroken loser.

- **Make sure it's a substantial flaw**, not just something cute such as being clumsy. It needs to be something that stops your protagonist from being fully happy, even though they'd never admit it.

- *Show* **that flaw or fear via action and dialogue instead of** *telling* **us about it.** Put your character in a situation that reveals their flaw, and then let readers draw their own conclusion instead of spelling everything out for them.

- You as the author have to know where that fear or flaw is coming from. Usually, it has to do with the character's backstory—for example, it could be a psychological wound from their childhood or past relationships. But don't succumb to the temptation to tell readers all about that backstory in the first act. For now, just **show us the effects of that wound in the present, and leave the backstory for later**.

- **Think ahead to act 2.** In the middle of the story, you will create a series of scenes that forces your protagonist to confront their misguided beliefs, fears, and flaws. In my novel *Just for Show*, Claire is confronted with the actress she hires for a fake relationship. Lana is a messy, overweight, out-of-work actress with scars and a tattoo. In short, she's the least perfect partner Claire can imagine. But the more she gets to know her, the more Claire realizes that perfection is overrated. She learns to accept her imperfections.

EXERCISE #40:

- Look at the same three novels from the last two chapters. Do the characters go through a transformation during the course of the books? What flaws and fears are revealed in the opening chapters? How did the authors reveal those flaws and fears?

EXERCISE #41:

- Now look at your own manuscript. Does your protagonist have a fear or flaw they'll have to overcome? If yes, did you establish that fear or flaw in the opening chapter? If you didn't, think about ways you could reveal that need for change. Could you use one of the techniques you found in exercise #40?
- If you are still planning your novel, what flaw or fear will you give your main character? How will you show readers that fear or flaw in the first chapter?

19. Task #10 —
How to foreshadow the end of the story

Remember that I told you not to worry too much about getting the beginning right during the first draft? That's because the most effective beginnings start with the end in mind, so once you know how your story ends, it will be easier to begin it the right way. The beginning needs to set up and foreshadow the end in some way.

PARTS OF ACT 3

Like the beginning (act 1), the ending of a book (act 3) consists of several parts. To connect beginnings and endings, only two parts are important:

- **The climax**: The protagonist and the antagonist (or antagonistic force) face each other in a final battle. This is where the main character either achieves their goal or fails—or they realize that they've been pursuing the wrong goal all along and no longer want it. In romance novels and other character-driven books, the antagonist is most often not a person but the protagonist's own fears or flaws, which they finally overcome in the story's climax.
- **The denouement**: Also called the resolution or aftermath, the denouement ties up loose ends in a final scene or two and shows what the protagonist's life looks like after the climactic scene.

HOW TO CONNECT YOUR BEGINNING TO THE ENDING

Here are a few options for how you can connect different parts of the beginning to hallmarks of the ending:

- **The climactic scene needs to answer the story question** that you've raised in the first act—will the detective catch the killer? Will the two main characters end up in a happy relationship? Will the protagonist be able to save earth from an alien attack?

- **In your story climax, the character proves that they have overcome their fear or flaw that has been set up in the opening.** For example, your first scene could show your protagonist unable to climb a ladder because they're afraid of heights. In the climax, they save the day by overcoming that fear.

- **Often, the opening scene and the final scene (denouement) will have some elements in common.** Both scenes could take place in the same place, or your protagonist could be in a similar situation. For example, the opening scene and the final scene of my historical romance *Hidden Truths* both start with the same line of dialogue, the main character shouting, "Run!"

- **Some elements of the ending will contrast with your beginning.** While the opening and the final scene might have some elements in common, there will also be differences. The circumstances might be similar, but the main character has changed. For example, the first and the final scene of my romance *Just for Show* both take place shortly before the guests arrive for the protagonist's engagement party. But while Claire rearranges the decorations and fusses with the buffet in the first scene, trying to get everything to look perfect, she's letting the caterers do their job in the final scene because she has learned throughout the book that appearances are overrated.

EXERCISE #43:

- Look at the opening and final scenes of three novels in your genre. Do they mirror each other in some way? Do they contrast in others?

EXERCISE #43:

- Now look at your own manuscript. Does your beginning reflect and contrast with the ending? Is your story question answered in the climax? Do you show the character's fear or flaw being overcome in the end?
- If you are still planning your novel, think about how you could connect your beginning to your ending. What elements could they have in common? What elements will be different and show the protagonist's growth?

PART IV —
The don'ts of writing a great beginning

After part III showed you all the things you need to do to write a great beginning, I'd now like to discuss the most common mistakes writers make when it comes to beginnings. When I recently sat down to analyze the opening chapters of submitted manuscripts I had rejected, I found the same patterns and issues over and over.

In this part, I'll share the results of my analysis with you. I'll teach you how to recognize and fix each of the common opening pitfalls. I'll give you an overview of the most common mistakes here and then go into more detail in the next chapters.

EXCEPTIONS

Before I get to my list of common mistakes, I should mention that there'll always be some exceptions. For each of the mistakes I list, you will probably be able to come up with an example of a best-selling book that committed exactly that mistake and still sold a lot of copies.

First of all, those books probably sold well *despite* and not *because of* the mistakes in their openings. Secondly, some authors are so incredibly talented that they might be able to pull off something that wouldn't work for the majority of writers. But unless you are already a best-selling author, the best advice for you is to avoid these mistakes.

20. The four most common mistakes in story beginnings —
How to avoid or fix these opening pitfalls

When I looked at my pile of rejected manuscripts with weak openings, I realized that their opening mistakes could be grouped into four categories: their openings were either too slow, confusing, misleading, or clichéd.

Each of these problems could be caused by several different issues in the manuscript. Here's an overview:

SLOW OPENINGS

The worst and most common offender among weak openings is a beginning that is overly slow. Too-slow openings can be caused by:

- Opening with an info dump
- Opening with backstory
- Opening with a lengthy description of the setting, the weather, or a character
- Starting the story too soon
- Opening with too much introspection
- Having a lack of conflict in the opening scene
- Not having a hook in the opening paragraph
- Being too wordy

CONFUSING OPENINGS

Sometimes in an attempt to not bore readers, writers go to the opposite extreme and cut too much context, leaving readers confused. Confusing openings most often result from:

- Opening the story too late
- Introducing too many characters in the opening scene
- Not grounding readers in the setting and time
- Not establishing the point of view right away
- Starting the story with unattributed dialogue
- Confusing readers with incorrect paragraph structure

MISLEADING OPENINGS

Remember when I said that the opening makes a promise to readers? When you break that promise, you create an opening that misleads readers. Misleading beginnings can be caused by:

- Writing in a tone that doesn't fit the rest of the story or its genre
- Starting the story with a dream or illusion

CLICHÉD OPENINGS

The fourth pitfall to avoid is a clichéd opening, for example:

- Opening with the main character waking up and going through their morning routine
- Opening with the main character traveling somewhere
- Having the character look in a mirror so you can describe them
- Opening with the protagonist introducing themselves

- Starting with any other opening that has been overused in your genre, for example, the first day of school in a YA novel, the characters falling instantly in love in a romance, or a medieval Europe-like setting in a fantasy novel

If you have made any—or all—of these mistakes, don't worry. I've made most of them at one point or another. The good thing is that all of these mistakes can be fixed. I'll show you how in the following chapters.

EXERCISE #44:

• Bookmark this page. Once you finish part IV of this guide, you can use it as a checklist to make sure you didn't make any of these common mistakes.

21. Overly slow openings I —
How to avoid info dumps

I'd say an overly slow opening is the most common mistake writers make in their opening chapters, and it's probably the number one reason for poor sales. If the beginning of the sample they are reading drags, readers will assume that the rest of the story is just as boring and put the book on their mental don't-buy list.

Of course, what is considered *too slow* depends on your genre. An action-packed thriller will obviously need a faster-paced opening than, let's say, a character-driven historical novel or an epic fantasy novel. I suggest you read extensively in your preferred genre to find out what the preferred pace for your target audience is. Checking out the best-selling, award-winning, and top-rated novels in your genre will give you a better idea of what your readers expect from a book like yours.

So what makes an opening too slow and boring? I'll focus on the most common reason—info dumps—in this chapter and then discuss other factors in the next chapter to keep each section at a length that is easy to digest.

INFO DUMPS

Some authors start their books with large blocks of information that they feel readers need to know to understand the story. This is called an info dump.

Most often, you'll find info dumps in the form of:

- **background information about the character**, their past, and how they got into this situation
- a lengthy **description of the setting or the weather**
- a lengthy **description of a character**
- an **explanation of the story world**, its history, politics, technology, or how the magic system works

Science fiction, fantasy, and historical novels are especially prone to info dumps, usually because writers have done a lot of research and world-building, and now they want to share the fruits of their labors with readers.

You'll also find info dumps in the openings of many classics. In the past, authors often opened their novels with long descriptions of the scenery or detailed information about their characters' pasts, sometimes even going back to when they were born. But that was a different time. Modern readers no longer have the patience to wade through long info dumps to get to the real story.

THE PROBLEM WITH INFO DUMPS

The problem with info dumps is that they are boring and static. It's all *telling*, not *showing*. There's nothing happening on the page to hook and engage readers. The characters aren't acting, interacting, or speaking.

Instead, the author is relaying information, and that's not what readers want. Readers are reading fiction because they want entertainment, not information. They want a story, so don't force them to read half a page of information or description to get to it.

Any time you insert an info dump, you stop the forward momentum of your story. It's as if you, the author, are holding up your hand, bringing the plot to a grinding halt, and saying, "Hang on, before we get back to the story, let me explain this one thing…"

HOW TO HAND OUT INFORMATION

If info dumps are bad, how are you supposed to give readers the information they need to understand the story? Here are a few tips:

- **Leave out information that isn't necessary.** For every piece of information you insert into the story, ask yourself: Do readers really need this information to understand the story? Does this detail move the story forward? Would leaving it out confuse readers?

- **Choose the best time to reveal each bit of information.** Generally speaking, the later, the better. Try to keep the opening chapter as free of explanations as possible. Ask yourself: Do readers need this information now, or can it wait until later in the story? Would it frustrate readers to leave this question unanswered for now?

- **Trust your readers.** They don't need as much information as you think they do to understand the story.

- **Gradually sprinkle in details.** Having to piece together the story themselves keeps readers actively engaged instead of being passively fed huge blocks of information.

- **Make the information part of the story** instead of something that stops the story. For example, instead of writing several paragraphs to explain how the weapon technology in your world works, give readers hints as your character starts to use a particular weapon.

> Arlen checked the *kharizat* crystals in his disruptor, reassured by their amber glow.

BACKSTORY

One common type of info dump is backstory. Backstory is everything that has happened before the opening line of your book. That includes the history of your world as well as your character backstory—their childhood and youth, family history, previous relationships, and old wounds.

THE PROBLEM WITH BACKSTORY

Backstory is important, of course. It's vital that you, the author, know what experiences in the past have shaped your characters and made them into who they are today because these events will influence their actions in the present. But that doesn't mean you have to tell readers the characters' entire life stories in the first three chapters.

Like other info dumps, backstory dumps stop the forward momentum of the story. Here's an example:

> Sarah sat on the bench, stretched out her legs, and looked around the park. Two old men were playing chess. A young woman was throwing a Frisbee to her dog, and several kids were laughing as they ran after a baseball.

> The whack of a bat hitting the baseball transported her back to her childhood. She raised her hand and touched the small scar on her forehead, where a baseball had hit her. She couldn't have been older than five or six, but she'd been determined to play baseball. She had begged her older brothers to let her join their game. They had always refused, until one day...

You can see how the backstory stops the action in the present cold and suddenly throws readers into a different story about little Sarah before we have even been given the chance to get to know adult Sarah in the present.

In addition to stopping the momentum of the story, a lot of backstory in the opening chapters is problematic for other reasons too:

• **Your readers want the story, not the backstory.** They want to be immersed into the action in the here and now, not read about events that happened in the past. By definition, backstory is all set in the past, so there's no action on the page for readers to become immersed in.

• **Readers need to care about characters first before they become interested in their past.** Getting too much information about a character readers don't yet care about can be annoying. It's a little like meeting a stranger at a party and they tell you their entire life story before you've even had a chance to catch their name. Let readers bond with a character in the present first before you give them any backstory.

- **Too much backstory ruins any sense of mystery and intrigue.** Getting to know characters slowly and discovering their pasts is part of the fun of reading. As I explained before, it's the unanswered questions that keep readers reading. If you give them all the information upfront, there's no reason for them to keep turning the pages.

HOW TO REVEAL BACKSTORY

However, backstory is important, so you need to insert it at some point. Here are some tips on how to do it without stopping the forward momentum of the story or causing any of the problems described above:

- **Keep backstory out of your opening chapter.** In your first chapter, focus on the here and now, and leave backstory for later.

- **Don't explain what happened to get your character into the current situation.** Sprinkle in the explanations later. If you really feel that readers need this information now, think about whether you are opening your story at the right point. Do readers need a paragraph of context before you hit them with the action?

- **Use the iceberg principle.** The majority of an iceberg is hidden beneath the water's surface, and only the tip is visible. It should be the same for character backstory. Most of what you know about the characters should stay hidden. Not every bit of information you know about the characters needs to make it into the story.

- **Cut out any backstory that isn't necessary.** For every bit of backstory, ask yourself: Do readers really need to know this to understand what's going on in this scene? Only let readers know character backstory if it is relevant to understanding their current actions. For example, in the

Harry Potter series, we have to know that Voldemort killed Harry's parents because it explains why Harry is so committed to his goal of defeating him.

- **Hint at backstory through objects, present behavior, or physical characteristics.** A lot of backstory can be implied instead of stated explicitly. For example, a character's scars can reveal past accidents, and photos on their bookshelf can show that they traveled extensively when they were younger. If your protagonist flinches when someone raises their voice, readers will assume that the character might have been in an abusive relationship in the past.

- **Make backstory part of the present action.** For example, instead of telling us about a character's past relationship, could we meet their ex-partner instead and see them interact so we can draw our own conclusions about their relationship?

- **Weave in backstory information in smaller bits as the story progresses.** Keep it to a sentence or two here and there instead of having the character think of the past for an entire page. That way, readers can get to know the characters the way they would people in real life: gradually.

- **Have a trigger for the backstory in the present.** Give your character a good reason to think about the past. For example, the scent of cinnamon reminds the protagonist of the cookies their grandmother used to make.

- **Find a natural place to insert the backstory.** Always ask yourself: Would my character really be thinking about this right now? Or is this bit of backstory actually a point of view violation? If your character angrily storms into their boss's office, where they have been a hundred times before, they probably wouldn't be thinking of the day their boss hired them. They would be focused on whatever made them angry right now.

- **Don't use flashbacks in the beginning.** A flashback can be one way to show a scene from the past, but I'd advise you to use that technique only later in the book (if at all), not in the first act. I'll explain the reasons in chapter 27.

- **Use a gradual revelation of backstory to hook readers.** Remember that unanswered questions can be a good thing because they keep readers turning the pages to find out the answers. Don't think you need to give readers all the information about why your character is acting in a certain way as soon as we see the action. Delay the answers and create a need within readers so by the time you drop in bits of backstory, they want to know. Drop in just enough backstory morsels to keep readers eager for more. For example, here's an excerpt from the first scene in which readers meet Rae, one of the main characters in my romance novel *The Roommate Arrangement*.

> Rae squinted into the darkness beyond The Fun Zone's front door, trying to keep watch on the people waiting in line. The glare of the flashing neon signs bothered her. She was already dreading driving home after the late show, but public transportation in LA was as shitty as her night vision, so there was no other option.
>
> Damn, she really needed to find an apartment within walking distance of the comedy club.

> *Not gonna happen. Stop whining and focus on work.*
>
> "Hey, newbie."
>
> The sudden voice seemingly out of nowhere sent her pulse skyrocketing, but she did her best to not let on that he had taken her by surprise and merely turned her head.
>
> One of her colleagues, Brandon Zimmerman, came into her field of vision. He had taken up position at the door right next to her.

Instead of explaining to readers that Rae lost one eye and telling them exactly how it happened, I give them hints that show that something isn't quite right with Rae's vision. They'll read on to find out what's wrong with her eyesight and how it happened.

- **Use dialogue to reveal backstory.** Give readers a glimpse into a character's past when another character finds out about it via dialogue. But please make sure it's information that the characters would naturally talk about in that scene. Avoid "as you know, Bob" dialogue, which is when one character tells another something they both already know, just so the author can inform the reader. Have another character present who doesn't already know this information and has a reason for asking these questions. Here's an example from my historical romance *Hidden Truths*:

> "Call me Phin." He reached for her hand and rested it in the crook of his elbow, then set

them off for a stroll along the corrals. "When you call me Phineas, I feel like my father is standin' behind me."

"And that wouldn't be a good thing?" Rika asked.

"No. My father was a real bastard." He blanched. "Um. Pardon my language."

- **Use backstory as bonding material.** Especially in a romance novel, one character revealing parts of their past to another can show the growing trust between them. However, make sure it happens at a natural pace. They wouldn't reveal their innermost secrets to each other the second time they talked.

- **Add conflict:** If you make one character reluctant to reveal information about their past, so the other character has to fight for it, finding out the backstory becomes exciting to readers.

- **Reveal backstory in emotional scenes.** Make backstory more interesting by having it come out when emotions run high. For example, instead of telling readers that your character's mother is an alcoholic and her sister doesn't help with their mom, you could show them arguing.

"Oh, come on! You have always been Mom's favorite!"

"Her favorite? No. I was the one who was *there*! I was there to help her into bed when she came

```
home drunk. I was there to clean up the vomit
when—"
```

```
"Yeah, yeah, I get it. You're the good daughter;
I'm the bad one."
```

LENGTHY DESCRIPTIONS

Lengthy descriptions of the setting, the weather, or the characters can be another form of info dump that slows down the story's pace to a crawl.

THE PROBLEM WITH LENGTHY DESCRIPTIONS

Of course, as we said in chapter 14, it's important to establish the time and place, but if you give readers too many details, they'll get overwhelmed and the story will get bogged down.

Also, opening with lengthy descriptive passages gives readers no character to bond with. Most readers read for the emotion, not for poetic descriptions of sunsets.

Setting and character descriptions are also mostly static. There's no action happening on the page to draw readers in. It's all still life, not a dynamic action shot.

HOW TO DESCRIBE YOUR SETTING

Here are a few tips that will help you avoid all these problems and make your setting descriptions as powerful as possible.

- As I mentioned in chapter 14, **give readers just enough detail to orient them to the time and place in the opening paragraphs**. Pick the most vivid details and cut the rest or leave it for later.

- **Don't stop the story while you describe the scenery.** Avoid stopping the action whenever a character enters a room so you can give readers a static description of the furniture. Instead, make the description part of the action. Have the character move through and interact with the setting.

    Static description, which stops the action:
    ```
    A large bookshelf stood to the left, and a
    pock-marked desk took up the back of the room.
    A plush, burgundy carpet covered the floor.
    ```

    Dynamic description, which is part of the action:
    ```
    Mark's foot sank into the burgundy carpet as he
    walked past the looming bookshelf to his left.
    He paused in front of the desk and trailed his
    finger over its pock-marked surface.
    ```

- **Use unique details.** Don't give readers a long, exhaustive (and exhausting) description of the setting. Instead, pick up to three details that are unique. What makes this office different from other offices? What sets this living room apart from other living rooms?

Here's the opening paragraph of *Tomorrow's Kin* by Nancy Kress:

```
The publication party was held in the dean's
office, which was supposed to be an honor. Oak-
paneled room, sherry in little glasses, small-
```

```
paned windows facing the quad—the room was
trying hard to be a Commons someplace like
Oxford or Cambridge, a task for which it was
several centuries too late.
```

The author doesn't tell us everything about the dean's office, but the three details she picked give us a vivid image. Notice that she also found a good way to let us know the book is set in the future.

- **Break up long blocks of description and weave them into the action in little bits and pieces.** Think about what details your POV character would notice right away and which might only register later.

- **Avoid opening the book with a weather report or a description of scenery.** If you do describe the weather or setting in your opening sentence, make sure you bring in a character in the next sentence to give readers some context and an emotional reaction to the description that they can identify with. For example:

```
Ash fell from the sky like gray snowflakes.
Sarah paused in the middle of Times Square
and squinted up at the sooty flakes. What the
hell?
```

- **Use dialogue to sneak in sections of description.** For example, your character could look around their hotel room and say, "Wow, I've seen bigger broom closets."

HOW TO DESCRIBE YOUR CHARACTERS

Descriptions of characters often suffer from the same problems as descriptions of the setting. Here is my advice on how to handle character descriptions:

- **Just as with setting descriptions, don't stop the action as soon as a new character shows up.** Instead of giving readers a head-to-toe description or a long list that includes hair color, eye color, height, and clothes, mention one or two of the most interesting details. Scatter other details throughout the story later.

- **Start with a detail that the POV character would notice from the distance,** then reveal more details such as eye color or an interesting mole when the POV character gets closer to the other character.

- **Describe physical details that reveal something about the character's personality, profession, or other background, not just about the way they look.** For example, does your character slouch because they're uncomfortable with their height? Do they have a very erect posture because they had ballet training?

- **Make sure your descriptions don't violate point of view.** I've recently edited a manuscript that opens with an entire paragraph describing the POV character's hair. People don't usually think about the way they look, so avoid having the POV character describe themselves—unless you give them a good reason to think about their appearance—for example, they are heading out on a date or a job interview or they just got a new haircut and are still getting used to it. Also, characters usually don't think about the appearance of people they are very familiar with. This description, for example, violates the character's point of view and slips into either an omniscient point of view or authorial intrusion:

> His father was a tall guy, even taller than Tom's six foot four, but he didn't have his burly build. He had blue eyes and blond hair and usually wore shorts, even in winter.

If you want to give readers an idea of how Tom's father looks, you have to get creative. You could, for example, have him duck when he enters a room, indicating that he's tall. Or maybe Tom hasn't seen him for a few months and notices that his blond hair is turning gray. But if his father looks the way he always does, Tom wouldn't stop to think about his appearance.

- Related to the previous point, **a character's description should reveal just as much about the POV character as it reveals about the person being described**. Here's an example from my romance novel *Something in the Wine*. The POV character is a winemaker, so she uses wine-related terms to describe the other character's hair color.

> Golden hair—the color of a fine, mature white wine—brushed against Annie's slender shoulders.

- **Instead of giving a static description, use active verbs and incorporate the description into the character's actions.** Here's an example:

Static description:
> Sarah had blonde, curly, unruly hair.

Dynamic description:

```
Sarah's blonde hair curled around her face.
She swiped a strand behind her ear, but it kept
falling across her cheek.
```

- **The amount of description you give a character should correlate to their importance in the story.** If you describe a character in detail, readers will assume they are a main character, so restrict the description of minor characters to a single detail.

- **Use dialogue for character descriptions**: Every now and then, you can even sneak some character description into your dialogue. Here's an example:

```
Sarah looked him up and down. "You look taller
on TV."
```

EXERCISE #45:

- Read the opening scene of three novels in your genre. How much information are the authors giving out? How are they doing it? Do you feel it's stopping the forward momentum of the story at any point? If the authors have managed to avoid that, what can you learn from the way they've handled giving out the information?

EXERCISE #46:

- Use the same three novels that you analyzed for exercise #45. How much information about the character's past do we find out in the opening chapters? How does the author reveal backstory—in dialogue, weaving it into the action in bits and pieces, or in blocks of information? Take note of what works and what doesn't.

EXERCISE #47:

- Look at the opening scene of the three novels again, this time focusing on descriptions of the setting, the weather, or characters. How much description is there? Are there any description dumps, or did the authors sprinkle in the descriptions gradually? Which descriptions worked particularly well for you, and what can you learn from it?

EXERCISE #48:

- If you haven't printed out your opening chapter yet, please do it now. Get three different colored highlighters. If you prefer to work on your computer, you can also use your writing software's text highlight function. Go over your opening scene and highlight backstory, descriptions of setting, weather, and characters, and other info dumps. For example, highlight backstory—all references relating to things that happened before the story began—in red. Highlight descriptions of the setting, the weather, or your characters in green. Highlight any other info dumps, such as explanations of technology or history, in blue. How much unmarked text—actions and dialogue in the present—now remains? If the highlighted sections dominate, try to cut out as much as you can until the majority of the text is unmarked. Copy the information you have decided to cut into a separate file as you might be able to use it later in the story. Leave only the information that readers need in order to understand the present action.

EXERCISE #49:

- After cutting any excess of backstory from your manuscript, look at the remaining parts of backstory. Use the "how to reveal backstory" list above as a checklist to revise your opening chapter.

EXERCISE #50:

- Now do the same for your setting and character descriptions. Use the "how to describe your setting" and the "how to describe your characters" lists above to make sure your remaining descriptions are as powerful as possible.

22. Overly slow openings II —
How to avoid other causes of dragging story beginnings

Once you have learned to fix info dumps and handle backstory and descriptions, you're a big step closer to your goal of creating a beginning that draws readers in and makes them want to read the rest of the book.

But there are other factors that could make your opening feel slow and boring. Here are a few other issues to avoid:

STARTING THE STORY TOO SOON

Novice authors often begin their stories way too early—meaning that they take too long before introducing the inciting incident. Their ordinary world section either goes on for too long or isn't interesting enough. Readers are forced to follow the main characters around while they go about their boring daily routine, and it takes much too long for anything interesting to happen.

Here are some red flags that might mean you have started your story too soon:

- **Your story starts with your character waking up** and doing everyday stuff such as getting dressed, having breakfast, or driving to work. Here's an example:

      Susan awoke to the sound of her bedside alarm
      clock. Her classes would be starting in an hour.
      Yawning, she climbed out of bed and headed to

> the bathroom. After taking a shower, she got
> dressed, then hastily made herself a sandwich
> and ate it while checking her email. Finally,
> she put on her coat, grabbed her backpack, and
> hurried out the door.

- **Your story starts with your character traveling somewhere**, usually while reflecting where they have been or what awaits them at their destination.

- **Your story starts with your character planning a trip.**

- **Your story starts with your protagonist getting ready for some event**, e.g., going out to a party.

My advice would be to cut most of those scenes. Start as close to the inciting incident as possible, and give readers only as much of the character's ordinary world as they really need.

For example:

- Instead of starting with the character waking up or driving to work, start with the character already at work, in the meeting where they find out they'll have to compete for the promotion they want.

- Instead of starting with the character traveling or planning a trip, start with them arriving at the new place.

- Instead of showing your character getting ready for the party, start with the character arriving at the party or already being at the party.

TOO MUCH INTROSPECTION

Another mistake I see quite often is a static opening in which the character thinks about their life while nothing interesting is going on for readers to engage with. That's the "sitting and thinking" problem I mentioned before.

This is often paired with the mistake I described above—opening the story too soon.

The character might be traveling somewhere or getting ready for work or a party, and while they are doing those mindless tasks, they will be reflecting on the past or their current situation. The problem is that you're presenting readers with static information instead of drawing them into the story with something interesting happening. All of the character's reflections are *telling*. Instead, *show* readers what's happening in the present.

Here's how to avoid bogging down your story with too much introspection:

- Is your character alone in the opening scene? If they are, **give them another character to interact with,** either in person or at least on the phone. Dialogue, interactions, and conflict are dynamic, and that's always more interesting than a static character who's just thinking about something.

- **Keep an eye out for too much internal monologue in the opening scene.** Are there any overly long passages of character thoughts? Some of them might be set off in italics, signaling direct character thoughts. Cut out some of them. Dip into the POV for a sentence or two every now and then, but otherwise, focus on the character's actions instead of keeping us in their head too much.

- **Don't allow your characters to talk to themselves** in the opening. That's not dialogue; that's thinking out loud and presents the same problems as too much introspection. Most often, it's just an excuse to dump information on your readers, plus it can make your character come across as slightly eccentric.

- Is your character doing something boring such as doing the dishes while thinking about their life? **Have them do something interesting** such as solving a problem.

LACK OF CONFLICT

Another common reason why the opening scene seems to drag is the lack of conflict. As I explained in chapter 17, your first scene must include some kind of conflict. Open the story with the character wanting something. A character with a goal turns a static, boring opening into a dynamic, interesting one, especially once you add conflict—something standing in the way of the character achieving their goal. Readers will want to read on to find out how the protagonist will attempt to solve the problem.

Here's an excerpt from the opening scene of my novel *Perfect Rhythm*. Pop star Leo is trying to convince her manager that she needs a break because she's close to burnout, but he doesn't want to listen.

> "How often do I have to tell you? I need a goddamn break." Her bare foot hit one of the stiletto boots, kicking it across the room.

Saul's new assistant winced. He probably thought she was some kind of diva throwing a tantrum, but she didn't care.

"Listen." Saul put his elbows on his thighs, leaned forward, and regarded her across the glass-topped coffee table. "I know you could do with a week of sipping cocktails on some tropical beach. By God, we all could. But you haven't had a number-one hit in more than three years."

A low growl rumbled in her throat. "I've spent half of those years on the road to promote my last album."

That clash of different goals makes for a more dynamic scene than if I had opened the book with Leo interacting with adoring fans and enjoying every second of it.

Whatever conflict you introduce in your opening scene, make sure to show it in action. Your character needs to encounter it in real time on the page, not just think about a problem that occurred earlier.

LACK OF A HOOK

The very first paragraph needs to hook us into the story. As I explained in chapter 10, we do that by creating questions in the reader's mind. The need to find out the answers is what will keep readers reading. If your opening doesn't spark any questions, you're not giving readers a reason to keep turning the pages.

Here's an example of an opening that could benefit from more of a hook:

> Gina leaned back in her high-backed leather chair, folded her arms behind her head, and gazed out the window. From her office, located on the fifteenth floor, the city looked picturesque. Gina's gaze tracked the boats in the harbor, as she had done every morning for the past year. Making partner at Snyder & Jennings was a dream come true.

As you probably realized, we have a character-is-sitting-and-thinking problem here. It would have been better to open with a client storming in or one of the partners handing her a new case or anything else that would have made readers ask at least one question.

WORDINESS

Sometimes, I'll come across an opening paragraph in a manuscript that has an interesting situation or problem, but it's buried beneath a ton of redundancies and extra words that don't contribute anything.

Here's an example:

> Charlotte pressed both hands to her pounding temples and walked quickly to the restroom. God, she had a splitting headache! She went to the sink, reached out with her right hand, and pulled several paper towels from the dispenser that hung on the tiled wall. She ran them under

```
cold water and leaned back against the sink as
she placed the cool, wet towels on the back of
her neck. Finally, the pain eased, causing her
to exhale in relief.
```

For readers, reading a paragraph like that feels like walking on a dry, sandy beach. At first, the extra effort required to walk on the sand isn't really noticeable. But after a while, the cumulative effort makes you feel tired and slow, as if it's taking forever to get anywhere and taking too much effort to do so.

Your story beginning, especially the opening scene, has to be written as tightly as possible. Every line—every word—must move the story forward. Leave out unnecessary details that slow down the pace of the story and lessen the impact of your hook.

For instance, the example above could be tightened and revised like this:

```
Charlotte stumbled to the restroom, both hands
pressed to her pounding temples. At the sink,
she ran several paper towels under cold water
and placed them on the back of her neck. As the
pain eased, she exhaled.
```

Here are a few **tips on how to tighten your writing**:

• **Weed out unnecessary details.** In the example above, it's irrelevant whether Charlotte pulls the paper towels from the dispenser with her right or her left hand.

• **Trust your reader to fill in the gaps.** I think it's safe to assume that your readers have been in a public restroom. They know that there are dispensers for paper towels and that they usually hang on the wall, so we could leave out those details too.

- **Use as few adjectives and adverbs as possible.** In the example above, it's already mentioned that she runs the paper towels under cold water, and we know water is wet, so we can cut the adjectives "wet" and "cool" without losing anything.

- **Avoid repeating yourself.** Are you giving readers the same information twice, just with slightly different words? In the example above, we already know Charlotte's temples are pounding, so we don't need her to tell us she has a splitting headache. Trust your readers to get it the first time.

- **Condense actions.** Look at the verbs, especially if you have more than three per sentence. Do you need to mention each action, or can some be assumed? Keep an eye on phrases such as "she reached out (a hand) and…" It's usually safe to leave that out.

- **Replace weak verb/adjective combinations with a stronger verb.** In the example above, I replaced "walked quickly" with "stumbled," which evokes an image in the reader's mind.

- **Avoid overly long, convoluted sentences and paragraphs.** Keep your sentences and paragraphs clear and on the shorter side on page 1.

- **Show, don't tell.** In most cases, showing is better than telling, and that's especially true for your opening scene. Showing keeps readers engaged because they have to actively interpret what they are reading, instead of the writer presenting them with conclusions. One of the red flags for telling that I point out in my book *Show, Don't Tell* is naming emotions. Whenever you find yourself using adjectives such as "surprised" or nouns such as "excitement," you are probably telling. Instead, *show* the character's emotions via thoughts, facial expressions, or body language. In the example above, I cut "in relief" because it was telling. Exhaling *showed* Charlotte's relief without having to add "in relief."

EXERCISE #51:

• Look at the opening scene of your manuscript. Is your character traveling somewhere, preparing for something, or going through their daily routine? If the answer is yes, cut those passages and start closer to the inciting incident or spice up the ordinary world section with interesting actions and conflict.

EXERCISE #52:

• Take another look at your opening scene. Is your protagonist alone? Would the scene become more interesting if you gave them another character to interact with?

EXERCISE #53:

• Get your printed-out manuscript and a highlighter again. Highlight any character thoughts and reflections in yellow. Is there too much of it in the opening scene? If there is, I suggest you cut some of it.

EXERCISE #54:

• Re-read the first scene of your manuscript. Does your protagonist have a goal in your opening scene? Do they encounter obstacles when trying to achieve that goal? If the answer is no, now's the time to revise and add some conflict to your scene. Feel free to re-read chapter 17 to help you with that.

EXERCISE #55:

• Read your opening paragraph and pretend you're a reader seeing it for the first time. What question would you want to have answered after reading the first paragraph? Is it a question that makes you curious enough to read on? If there's no clear question being raised, revise your opening to include a stronger hook. If you'd like, re-read chapter 10.

EXERCISE #56:

- Go over your opening scene and cut any unnecessary words. Keep an eye out for adjectives, adverbs, weak verbs, and sentences that go on for too long. Pay special attention to your opening paragraph, and make sure every word moves the story forward.

23. Confusing openings —
How to avoid puzzling readers

Having a too-slow opening because of issues such as info dumps isn't the only common problem, though. Sometimes, authors go too far in the other direction and provide too little information, leaving readers confused. A puzzled reader is just as likely to put the book down and never pick it up again as a bored reader.

In this chapter, I'll explain the most common causes of confusing openings and teach you how to avoid or fix them.

FAILING TO ANSWER READER QUESTIONS

In chapter 9, I explained that readers approach each story with questions they need to have answered so they can settle into the story and enjoy the ride. If your first few paragraphs fail to answer those questions, your readers will get confused.

I'm not talking about the unanswered questions you're putting into the story on purpose, to hook your readers. I'm talking about questions readers need to have answered to orient themselves in the story world and be sure that this is the kind of book they want to read.

The most important of these questions:

1. **What kind of story is this?** Readers want to know the novel's genre and overall tone. Is it a historical romance or a cozy mystery? Is it serious or funny? Chapter 13 gave you important pointers on how to establish your novel's tone.

2. **Whose story is this?** Readers want to know right away who the protagonist is.
3. **Who is telling this story?** Readers want to know whose point of view they are in.
4. **When and where does the story take place?** Readers want to know the time and place of the events.

I'll talk more about some of these questions in the next section.

OPENING THE STORY TOO LATE

While some writers start their story too early, giving readers copious pages of the character in their everyday life while nothing exciting is happening, some writers go too far in the opposite direction and start the story too late.

Maybe because they've been told to "start with action," they open their book in the middle of an action scene. The problem with that is that readers have no context to understand the situation. They don't know who the characters are, what they are doing, or why they should care whether they live or die. Readers feel lost, struggling to understand.

Here's an example:

```
River's blade slashed through the air, aiming
for Yolas's throat.

He parried the strike at the last moment.
Before he could recover, Valuca jumped into
the fight.
```

```
Yolas twirled his sword around, but Valuca
sidestepped, nearly crashing into River in the
process.
```

In this scene, we have no idea who we're supposed to be rooting for, who attacked whom and why, where they are, and why we should care about the outcome of the fight. It could be a mugging, the middle of a battle, or a practice fight between friends that someone took a little too far.

In this case, it might have been better to back up a little and take a paragraph or two to show Yolas (assuming he's the protagonist) going about his business and then have two attackers jump out at him. There could be a few lines of dialogue that shows us what they are after—revenge, money, or something else—before the fight begins.

INTRODUCING TOO MANY CHARACTERS

Part of what made the sword fight example in the previous section so confusing was the fact that the opening immediately introduced three characters by name, yet we have no idea who they are or which one is the protagonist.

Here are a few tips on how to avoid confusing readers with too many characters:

• **Limit the number of characters you introduce in your opening scene.** While your main character shouldn't be alone—sitting and thinking—you don't want to go to the other extreme and throw too many characters at your readers. It's like being introduced to dozens of people at a party. You will probably end up forgetting their names or mixing up all the information you learn about them. I'd suggest introducing no more than three characters in the first scene.

146

- It's not just about the people who are present in the opening scene. Also **avoid having your character think about several characters who aren't in the room**. These characters count toward your three-character limit in the first scene.

- **Start the story with your protagonist.** Readers will assume that the very first character they meet is the one they're supposed to root for. If possible, have the first name that is mentioned be the name of the protagonist.

- **Avoid opening the book with a group activity scene** such as a party.

- **Cut unnecessary characters from the opening scene.** Here's an example:

  ```
  Sarah's stomach rumbled as she strolled toward
  the cafeteria.

  A young man with a laptop bag strapped across
  his chest nodded at her as he walked past and
  gave her a quick smile.
  ```

Unless that young man will turn out to be important, I'd cut him from the opening scene completely and focus on Sarah and what happens once she enters the cafeteria.

- **Don't name unimportant characters.** If you give characters a name and describe them, readers will assume they are going to be important. In the opening scene, the barista who makes your protagonist's latte should remain an unnamed extra.

- **Make sure your characters' names are not too similar.** If you have a character who's named Anja and another who's named Anita, they are easy to confuse. Don't have names that rhyme, e.g., Jim and Tim, and don't use names that start or end with the same letter or sound, e.g., Brandy, Carrie, and Jenny. For more advice on how to name your characters, check out these twelve tips on my blog.

NOT GROUNDING READERS IN PLACE AND TIME

While you shouldn't open your book with long-winded descriptions of your setting, it's important to establish the time and place right away, as discussed in chapter 14. Nothing is more confusing than not knowing where you are. That was another problem the sword fight example had in the previous section. There wasn't a single detail that let us know the time or place. The names and the fact that the characters were using swords led us to assume that we were not in the present, but the setting could be a medieval world or a fantasy one set in the future. We could be on a faraway planet or in an alley of a thirteenth-century city, but we simply don't know.

Find the right balance: don't bog your story down with too many details, but give your readers just enough information so they are able to create a mental image of where the scene is taking place. Pick a couple of specific details, and don't forget to use the five senses to immerse readers into your story world.

NOT ESTABLISHING A POV

To avoid confusing readers, let them know right away whose head they are in. Avoid opening your novel without a clear point of view, as it happens often in books that start with a description. Here's an example:

> Tim poured gravy over the pile of mashed potatoes on his plate.
>
> "You really had no idea your parents were coming?" Sarah took the gravy from him.
>
> "Why should I?" Tim asked.
>
> Sarah stabbed at a carrot with her fork. "They're your parents!"

All we get is dialogue and actions, without any emotions or thoughts. There's no clearly established point of view. While you shouldn't overdo the introspection, try to dip into the POV character's head early on.

Here's a possible rewrite of the example above:

> Sarah squinted at the heap of mashed potatoes on Tim's plate. *So much for no carbs after six.*
>
> Tim poured gravy on his mashed potatoes.
>
> "You really had no idea your parents were coming?" Sarah took the gravy away from him before the puddle on his plate could become an ocean.
>
> "Why should I?" Tim asked.
>
> Sarah stabbed at a carrot with her fork. "They're your parents!"

DIALOGUE WITH NO CONTEXT

Some editors will tell you not to open with dialogue because readers have no context for the conversation. They don't know who's talking and to whom.

Personally, I think opening with a line of dialogue can work really well—if you do it the right way. Dialogue is showing; it's immediate, and the way people talk and what they say will reveal a lot about their personality.

But if you decide to open your book with dialogue, you have to establish a context right away so readers don't become confused. Here's how to do it:

- **Don't open with unattributed dialogue.** Use a dialogue tag to let your readers know who's talking right away. Action beats can also give readers clues as to who's speaking. For example:

  Dialogue tag: "Give me that," Sarah said.
  Action beat: "Give me that." Sarah wiggled her fingers at the package of cookies.

- **Avoid talking heads syndrome.** Talking heads syndrome happens when you have a dialogue-heavy scene with little or no description of where the characters are or what they are doing. The characters seem to be merely talking heads floating in empty space. Here's an example:

  "Give me that," Sarah said.

  "Nope," Tim answered.

"Give me those cookies!"

"Why should I?"

"Because I know where you keep the M&M's."

Even if you write mostly dialogue in your first draft, go back during the revisions and flesh out the scene by adding a bit of context—a setting detail or an action beat here, an inner reaction from a character there. Anchor your readers in the physical world and help them visualize what the characters are doing while they talk.

Here's how the example above could look after fleshing it out:

"Give me that." Sarah wiggled her fingers at the package of Oreos.

Tim dropped onto the couch and cradled the cookies to his chest. "Nope."

"Give me those cookies!"

He smirked up at her. "Why should I?"

Sarah rounded the coffee table, towered over him, and aimed for her most menacing tone as she said, "Because I know where you keep the M&M's."

- **Make your dialogue easy to follow by using correct paragraph structure.** Read on to find out how to structure your paragraphs the right way.

INCORRECT PARAGRAPH STRUCTURE

The majority of writers whose submissions come across my desk clearly have no idea about paragraph structure. You might think that's a really small, comparatively unimportant issue, but it's actually not.

Think about the functions of paragraphs for a second.

- **Paragraphs provide structure and make it easier to follow the story.** They group sentences that belong together and separate them from sentences that don't belong together.

- **Paragraphs help readers keep track of who's talking**, so if a writer structures paragraphs correctly, a lot of dialogue tags can be cut.

- **Paragraphs help with pacing.** Short paragraphs make readers' gazes move down the page faster and so they speed up the pace of the story, while longer paragraphs slow the pace.

- **Paragraphs create white space on the page.** If readers look at a book and see a page that is basically one big block of dense text, they're less likely to want to read that book because it looks overwhelming. Remember that most readers nowadays read e-books on small-screen devices, so breaking up the text into paragraphs becomes even more important—but those paragraph breaks need to be in the right places.

Here are some simple rules of thumb:

- **Everything one character says, does, and thinks belongs in the same paragraph.** If you separate a character's actions from their dialogue, readers will think the dialogue belongs to a different character.

- **For the dialogue or actions of another character, start a new paragraph.** Here's an example:

  Incorrect paragraphing:
  "If you stick to my advice, your numbers should improve within the next six months."

  Sarah handed him the documents. Tim put them into his briefcase and stood.

  "Thanks. I'll let you know how things go," he told Sarah.

  Correct paragraphing:
  "If you stick to my advice, your numbers should improve within the next six months." Sarah handed him the documents.

  Tim put them into his briefcase and stood. "Thanks. I'll let you know how things go."

You'll notice the correct paragraph structure makes the dialogue tag "he told Sarah" unnecessary because the action beat (Tim put them into his briefcase…) already identifies who's speaking.

- **Start a new paragraph when you move forward or backward in time.** Here's an example:

  Sarah slammed the driver's side door, started the engine, and stepped on the gas.

  Twenty minutes later, she parked the car in front of her parents' house.

EXERCISE #57:

- Look at the first few paragraphs of your manuscript. Are you opening in the middle of an action scene that could confuse readers? Think about ways to revise these lines so that you can give readers some context and help them understand what's going on.

EXERCISE #58:

- Re-read your opening scene. How many characters have you introduced? How many are named? If there are more than three characters mentioned, are there any you could leave out or at least not introduce by name? Start a list of names. Are any of them too similar to each other? If they are, rename one of the characters.

EXERCISE #59:

- Take a look at your first three paragraphs. Are you giving readers enough details to ground them in time and place? Don't go overboard, but if you think readers could be confused about the time and setting, add a specific detail or two.

EXERCISE #60:

- Re-read your opening paragraphs. Are there any clues that let us know whose point of view we are in? If you have a very objective first paragraph with only actions, dialogue, and descriptions, subtly dip into the POV character's head to reveal their emotions or thoughts within the first paragraph.

EXERCISE #61:

- Look at the dialogue in your first three paragraphs. Is there any? Is it clear right away who's talking? Did you provide enough action beats and little sensory details to avoid the talking heads syndrome? If you didn't, add those details now, but avoid going overboard.

EXERCISE #62:

• Take a look at the paragraph structure in your first scene. Are you using paragraph breaks in the correct places, keeping actions and dialogue from one character together, but separating them from the actions and dialogue of other characters? Revise until you are sure your paragraph breaks are in the right places. Are there any dialogue tags that have now become unnecessary?

24. Misleading openings —
How to avoid making readers feel cheated

As I mentioned before, your beginning is a promise to your readers. The opening lets readers know what kind of story to expect. If your beginning misleads them into assuming something about the book that then turns out to be wrong, you are breaking that promise. Your readers will feel as if you cheated them, and that's definitely not something you want.

In this chapter, I'll tell you how to avoid misleading your readers.

OPENING IN A TONE THAT DOESN'T FIT THE GENRE

Each genre comes with certain expectations. Fans of mystery novels expect a certain tone, which will be different from the tone that is typical for romance novels. If you write your opening in a style and tone that makes readers think "mystery," you'll attract mystery readers. If your book then turns out to be a romance, the typical mystery reader will be disappointed and annoyed.

Make sure your story beginning fits its genre and matches the tone in the rest of the book. Don't pick a slow, reflective opening for a thriller or start your romantic comedy with a gruesome murder.

Here's an example from a sports romance I recently beta read:

> A tickle of warm breeze lifted a few loose
> strands of hair underneath Morgan's ponytail.

> Somewhere behind her someone coughed, and to her right the creek in front of the green gurgled as it trundled over the bedrock.

While there's nothing fundamentally wrong with this opening, it doesn't exactly scream *sports romance*, does it? It could be a description of a picnic in a park on a lazy Sunday afternoon. Sports romance fans want to see the athlete character compete and experience their drive to win right away.

The author ended up cutting the first paragraph and starting the story with the second one:

> A bead of sweat tracked its way down Morgan's neck. She exhaled slowly and tried to relax her tight shoulders.
>
> Ten feet. That's all this putt was. Ten feet between her and a playoff for a chance to win the first major of her career.
>
> *But you've been this close before*, a nasty little voice whispered in her head. *Twice. And each time you blew it.*

That gives the character a goal and introduces conflict—her own self-doubts—right away, which makes for a dynamic opening that fits a sports romance.

STARTING WITH A DREAM OR ILLUSION

If you have ever opened a story or a chapter with the character dreaming and then waking up, you're not alone. A lot of writers make that classic mistake. I know I have done it. I thought it was a clever twist, but the problem is that dreams create a false beginning.

Readers will assume whatever is happening in the dream is real, so they'll get invested in what they think is the character's reality. But then the character wakes up, and it all turns out to have been a dream. Not only will readers feel deceived, but you are also forcing them to start the story a second time and become invested in a new reality, after having been ripped out of the first scenario.

Opening with a dream can be especially problematic if the dream situation is full of action, drama, and conflict, capturing the reader's interest. If you then have the character wake up and go through their morning routine, the reality will seem boring in comparison to the dream world you created.

If you do decide to open your story—or any scene later in the book— with a dream, don't let readers think it's real. Find a way to let them know right away that it's a dream.

Here's an example of a dream sequence that works because it doesn't cheat readers. It's from *Dreamlander* by K.M. Weiland:

> Dreams weren't supposed to be able to kill you. But this one was sure trying its best.

STARTING WITH A GIMMICKY HOOK

In an attempt to hook their readers or to start with action, some writers create a gimmicky hook. They open with a scene in which the protagonist seems to be fighting for their life—but then it's revealed that it was all just a video game. Or the book starts with what we think is the main character being stalked by a serial killer—but then we find out it's just her hot neighbor trying to ask her out.

Dream sequences belong in the "gimmicky hook" category too, and the problem with this type of opening is always the same: readers become involved in an action-filled reality—and then find out it doesn't exist.

Hooks like that promise readers a suspenseful story, but then breaks that promise when the character wakes up and the book turns out to be a romance or some other type of book.

KILLING OFF A CHARACTER READERS ASSUMED TO BE THE PROTAGONIST

Another kind of false beginning creates an incorrect expectation about who the main character is. If you open in the point of view of a character and then have readers follow them around for a scene or even an entire chapter, readers will assume that character to be the protagonist.

If you then kill off that character, readers will feel cheated. You are forcing them to start the story over with a different protagonist, after having invested their emotions into another character. Many readers won't be willing to do that. So if you are going to kill off a character, make sure it's clear from the start that they are only a minor character.

TV shows and mystery series can often get away with starting the book in the victim's point of view because the audience is already familiar with the main character and the format of the series or show. They expect the character in the opening scene to be killed off so the protagonist can come in and investigate the murder. But even then, the author of such a series usually kills off the victim right away so readers won't start to bond with the wrong character.

EXERCISE #63:

- Print out the first scene of your manuscript and give it to three people who haven't read it before. Have them guess the genre of your book just from this first page. Did they get it right? If most of them guessed wrong, the tone of your opening scene might not be right for the book's genre.

EXERCISE #64:

- Did you open your story (or a chapter later in the book) with a dream sequence? If you did, did you let readers know right away that it's just a dream, not a reality to get invested in? If you didn't, revise the scene right now—or maybe cut it entirely and start with something else.

EXERCISE #65:

- Take a long, hard look at your opening chapter. Is there anything else in there that might mislead readers? Did you kill off any characters? Did you create a situation that turns out to be different from what readers assumed? If the answer to any of these questions is yes, is that plotline really a clever twist or did you promise readers a story you are not delivering, forcing them to basically start the story twice?

25. Clichéd openings —
How to avoid overdone beginnings

Certain story beginnings have been used in so many books and movies that they have become clichés. That includes some of the mistakes I have discussed in earlier chapters, e.g., starting with the protagonist dreaming, waking up, or traveling somewhere. If you want your book to stand out from the masses of similar books, you must avoid these clichés—or give them a fresh twist.

Here's a list of additional clichés to be aware of in your opening chapters:

- **Opening with the character looking in a mirror** so you can describe them. I bet you have read more than one book in which the author has the character look into a mirror—or some other reflective surface such as a window or a lake—and then think about her blonde tresses or green eyes. That's not only overdone, it's also a POV violation, so please avoid it not just in your opening chapter but in the rest of the book as well. Find more creative ways to describe your protagonist.

- **Opening with a first-person narrator introducing themselves.** In genres such as young adult, so many books open with the narrator talking directly to the reader ("my name is…") that it has become a cliché.

- **Opening with a phone call,** especially a character being awakened by a phone call.

- **Opening with a battle scene** or the aftermath of a battle.

- **Opening with the character being chased** and running from something. Running through a forest seems to be especially overused.

- **Opening with the character moving to a new town** after a divorce.

- **Opening with a funeral.** The book opens with the protagonist standing at a graveside or attending a wake.

- **Opening with the protagonist suffering from amnesia**, wondering who they are.

Readers have seen these beginnings so often that they are starting to feel unoriginal. Don't get me wrong; I'm not saying you can never use them—well, except for the dream opening and the mirror description. Definitely avoid these at all costs. For the rest, my advice would be to either avoid them or try to write them with a fresh perspective and give them a unique spin.

AVOID GENRE-SPECIFIC CLICHÉS

In addition to these overused openings, every genre has its own clichés.

- **In romance novels**, two of the worst clichés are insta-love—the two characters instantly falling in deep, everlasting love at first sight—and the "meet cute" where the two main characters literally bump into each other, causing one of them to spill their drink or drop a stack of files or whatever else they've been carrying.

- **In paranormal fiction**, starting with the protagonist dying and being turned into a vampire, zombie, or werewolf might be done to…um, death.

- **In mysteries**, the alcoholic detective arriving at the crime scene hungover or the tough private investigator being hired by a hot, mysterious client might be overdone too.

- **In fantasy novels**, a world populated by elves and other creatures from *The Lord of the Rings*, a bearded, wise, old mentor, and an orphaned protagonist who'll turn out to be the heir or heiress to the throne are often considered clichés.

- **In science fiction novels**, the protagonist being woken by the spaceship's alarms going off is used a lot.

- **In young adult novels**, a book beginning on the first day at a new school is starting to feel like a worn-out cliché.

A set of fresh eyes can be really helpful to avoid clichés like these, so I'd recommend looking for beta readers who are avid readers in your genre and who know what has been done a thousand times before.

EXERCISE #66:

- Use the lists above to check your story beginning for clichés. Do you have a dream sequence or a character looking into a mirror in your opening chapter? Are you using any of the genre-specific clichés?

EXERCISE #67:

- Think about openings you have seen a lot in your genre. Make a list of clichéd elements that you want to avoid in your opening chapters.

PART V —
Three types of openings to avoid

When I looked at the pile of manuscripts my publishing house had rejected due to their poor openings, I found they not only contained one or more of the common mistakes I explained in part IV, many of the submissions also started with openings that rarely work—a prologue, a flashback, or a flash-forward.

In this part, I'll explain why most of the time it's not a good idea to start with these three types of openings and how to make it work if you feel you absolutely have to.

26. Prologues —
Why you should avoid prologues (most of the time) and how to make one work

A prologue is a passage that appears before the first chapter, set off from the rest of the book. It often takes place outside of the timeframe of the novel—years, decades, or even centuries before (or sometimes after) the events in chapter 1.

Prologues are frequently told from the point of view of a character who isn't the protagonist, sometimes even a character who might not get their own POV in the story again.

Prologues are so common in genres such as science fiction and fantasy that they almost seem like a cliché of their own. In other genres such as young adult or contemporary romance, prologues are rare.

Many readers, editors, and literary agents hate prologues. Some skip them, and there are readers who will refuse to buy a book as soon as they see the word "prologue."

Yet many writers insist on using them because they are convinced that their prologue is different and that it needs to be included because it reveals information readers need to understand their story.

Here's my advice on prologues: Don't use them unless it's absolutely necessary. Most prologues aren't, no matter what the book's author might think.

I'm not saying that prologues can never work. Every now and then, I find one that does. But most of the time, you're better off without a prologue and you don't really need it.

THE PROBLEM WITH PROLOGUES

But don't just take my word for it. Read through this list of problems prologues cause, and then decide for yourself if using a prologue is a good idea.

- **Prologues are often just info dumps.** The worst type of prologue is a three-page essay that explains the story world and its history. Remember that your readers want a story, not an abundance of information. Instead of dumping a prologue full of information on them, start with chapter 1 and weave in your world-building details gradually as the story progresses. Let your readers discover your world and experience it along with the characters.

- **Prologues force readers to start the story twice.** For you, that means you will have to hook them twice.

- **Prologues often feature a character who isn't the protagonist.** As I explained before, readers will usually bond with the first character they meet, so it's better to start with your protagonist than with a character they might not even meet again.

- **Switching time, place, and point of view in chapter 1 will lose many readers.** The abrupt shift between the prologue and chapter 1 will jar a lot of readers out of the story because they aren't grounded in the story yet.

- **Sometimes, prologues aren't representative of the book since they are written in a tone and style that doesn't match the rest of the story.** Remember that the beginning of the story makes a promise to readers, and then the rest of the book must keep that promise, and that's hard to do if your prologue differs from chapter 1 in style and tone.

- **Prologues can feel like false beginnings** if they are completely different from the rest of the book, making readers feel misled.

- **Prologues can make your story feel like a consolation prize.** If you manage to write a prologue that is riveting, readers will get invested in that story and want to continue reading it. When they get chapter 1 instead, they could decide that the real story isn't as intriguing and stop reading.

WHEN NOT TO USE A PROLOGUE

In general, I think most books don't need a prologue. But you especially should not use a prologue for the following:

- **To give information or backstory to readers.** Whatever you do, don't make your prologue a giant info dump. Most of the time, you'll be able to find ways to share that information with readers throughout the story. If you can't find a way to put the information later in the story, maybe it doesn't need to be in the book at all.

- **To create a certain mood.** If the sole purpose of your prologue is creating a certain atmosphere, it's not doing enough. You can easily do that in chapter 1.

- **To spice up your beginning.** Some authors use an action-packed, mysterious, or otherwise fascinating prologue because they know their first chapter is boring. Here's the thing: even if you tack on a great prologue, your first chapter will still be boring. Instead of using a prologue as a hook, revise chapter 1 to make it more interesting. Chapters 21 and 22 of this guide will give you some pointers.

WHEN TO USE A PROLOGUE AFTER ALL

Every now and then, a prologue can really work. Here are a few reasons for when you might want to use a prologue after all:

- **To give readers *essential* information that you can't give them *any other way.*** Please notice the emphasis on *essential* and *any other way.* It must be information that readers need in order to understand the story and that you can't reveal any other way. It could be something your protagonist doesn't know about, so you can't show it in their point of view. For example, mysteries, crime novels, and thrillers often start with a prologue from the villain's or sometimes the victim's point of view. The prologue reveals the threat of a killer on the loose before the main character knows about it, which creates tension and suspense. If you're not sure whether the information revealed in the prologue is essential or not, give chapter 1 to a couple of readers and see if they can follow the story without the prologue.

- **To set the right expectations.** If chapter 1 doesn't clearly give readers the right idea about what kind of book it's going to be, a prologue can help set the right expectations. For example, if not for its prologue, *Star Wars: Episode IV – A New Hope* would open with Luke's life as a farmer on a desert planet. The prologue shows a space battle between the rebels and Darth Vader's troops, so that's a better indication of what the movie is about.

PROLOGUE OR CHAPTER 1?

Before you title the opening section of your novel *prologue*, ask yourself: Is it really a prologue, or is it a misnamed first chapter?

A true prologue is usually separated from the main structure of the book by taking place in another time or being told from a different point of view. There must be a distinct shift from the prologue to chapter 1. If your prologue flows seamlessly into chapter 1 without any switch, rename your prologue *chapter 1*.

NECESSARY OR NOT?

If you are playing with the idea of starting your book with a prologue, your only criteria should be: Is it necessary or not? Here are a few questions to help you find out:

- **Is the information in the prologue really necessary for readers to have?** Skip the prologue for now and see if the story works without it. If you are too close to your work to judge it objectively, give your manuscript to a couple of test readers without the prologue. Do they think chapter 1 works fine without it? Can they follow the story without any problems?

- **Is it absolutely impossible to convey the information in another way?** If you could reveal the information throughout the story, ideally in small chunks, that's always a better choice.

- **Does your prologue have a different POV character or is set in a different time or place compared to the rest of the book?** If the prologue fits in with the rest of the book, it's not a prologue; it's your first chapter.

Only if you answered "yes" to all of these questions should you even consider starting your book with a prologue.

TIPS FOR WRITING A PROLOGUE

Let's assume you've decided you absolutely must start your book with a prologue, despite all the disadvantages and problems that come with it. If you feel you must write a prologue, here are some tips on how to make it effective:

- **Make sure it's not an info dump.** Your prologue shouldn't read like an essay about the history, politics, or society of your world. My advice in chapter 21 on how to avoid info dumps and backstory dumps is valid for prologues too.

- **Show, don't tell.** Your prologue needs to be a dramatized scene with characters, action, conflict, and dialogue, not just the narrator or author giving out information about the character or the world. There's one exception to this piece of advice: some prologues are written in the form of a (usually fictional) document such as a newspaper article, a blog post, a diary entry, a poem, a song, or a letter. While this kind of prologue doesn't need to be dramatized, all the other rules still apply.

- **Keep it short.** Readers want the real story to start as soon as possible, so keep your prologue to a single scene that isn't longer than a page or two.

- **Make sure the events in the prologue are relevant to the rest of the story.** They need to affect the plot in a substantial way. That's what makes prologues tricky: they need to be a strong part of the story, yet stand apart from it too. The sooner it becomes obvious how the prologue ties in with the main story and how the events in the prologue affect the protagonist, the better. For example, the prologue in *The Pillars of the Earth* by Ken Follett works really well. It depicts the hanging of a man for theft, even though there are some questions about him having been set up. The prologue ends with a young girl in the crowd cursing the men who condemned him, and readers can sense right away that the curse will be important to the story.

- **Make it interesting and include hooks.** Your prologue needs to catch readers' attention right away, so make sure it begins on a hook and ends on a hook too. Leave the reader with an intriguing question that they expect to have answered as they continue reading. *The Pillars of the Earth* by Ken Follett starts with the line *The small boys came early to the hanging* and leaves readers wondering if an innocent man has been hanged and what will happen to the cursed men.

- **Set the prologue apart from the rest of the book**, for example, by giving it a different point of view character or setting it at a different time.

- **Match the tone and the style to the rest of the story.** Make sure the prologue and chapter 1 don't feel as if they are parts of two different books. For example, if your book is written in third-person limited point of view, don't write your prologue in an omniscient point of view.

- **Make sure chapter 1 is just as intriguing as the prologue** so readers won't lose interest. While the prologue should be interesting, it shouldn't overpower your first chapter. Start chapter 1 with a hook that is just as strong as the one in your prologue.

EXERCISE #68:

- Think about your own attitude toward prologues as a reader. Do you read them, skip them, scan them? Can you think of examples of prologues you enjoyed? What made them work for you?

EXERCISE #69:

- If you started your book with a prologue, run it through the checklist above to see if it's necessary. Try cutting the prologue. Does chapter 1 still make sense? Is it possible to weave the information you relay in the prologue into the story as it progresses?
- If you are still unsure whether you need the prologue, give your manuscript to a couple of test or beta readers without the prologue. Did they still understand and enjoy the story? If they did, I'd suggest cutting the prologue.

27. Flashbacks —
Why you shouldn't use a flashback in your story opening

You have probably heard of flashbacks and maybe even used them in your story. Before I tell you why you shouldn't use them in your opening chapters, let's take a closer look at what flashbacks are—and what they aren't.

FLASHBACK VS. MEMORY

Both flashbacks and memories are ways to get backstory across to readers, but these two techniques are not the same:

- **Flashbacks** *show* an event from the character's past in a fully fleshed-out, *dramatized* scene, including actions, dialogue, and sensory details. Readers are taken back into the past and experience it as if it were happening in real time.

- **Memories** *tell* readers about an event from the character's past and *summarize* what happened. The POV character is thinking about something that happened in the past while they remain in the present. Here's an example:

      Sarah put her arms behind her head and looked
      around her old room, remembering that day
      fifteen years ago when her father had barged
      into the room and told her to leave and never
      come back. She had fled the house with just
      enough money for a bus ticket to Baltimore.

Yet here she was, back in her childhood bedroom.

In a fully dramatized flashback, readers would have seen the entire scene play out as if it were happening right now and witnessed the dialogue between Sarah and her father instead of getting a two-sentence summary.

FLASHBACK VS. PROLOGUE

Flashbacks are different from prologues set in the past; they flash back from a scene set in the present, while that type of prologue starts in the past and doesn't disrupt the chronological sequence of the story.

THE PROBLEM WITH FLASHBACKS

Since flashbacks *show* instead of *tell*, you might think they are a great way to reveal backstory, but they come with their own set of problems. Some of them are similar to the problems prologues can cause.

- **Flashbacks are backstory.** They show a scene from the past, but readers want to see what happens in the present. When you insert a flashback into your story, you risk annoying readers who want to know what happens next, not what has happened in the past.

- **Flashbacks stop the forward momentum of the plot** and jerk readers out of the flow of the story. A lot of the time, sneaking in a short memory—just a sentence or two—might be better than taking the reader away from the action in the present for an entire flashback scene.

- If the transition into and out of flashbacks isn't handled skillfully, **the jumps back and forth in time can be disorienting and confuse readers.**

Using flashbacks can be problematic at any time, but having a flashback in the opening chapters of your story comes with additional problems:

- **Readers don't want to hear about the character's past yet.** In the opening chapters, readers don't know or care about the character yet, so they aren't interested in their past.

- **Readers aren't yet grounded in the here and now of the story**, so any interruption of the chronological sequence can jar them out of the story.

- **Flashbacks that happen too early kill the mystery.** As I have already mentioned several times, it's the unanswered questions that keep readers turning the pages. If you reveal backstory via flashback too soon and answer all of those questions, readers have no reason to keep reading. For example, in my romance *The Roommate Arrangement*, Steph notices that Rae always sits with her back to the wall, keeping the exit in her view. But there's no flashback that reveals why, so readers read on to find out.

Given all these problems, here's my advice on flashbacks: Don't use them until you have given your readers enough time to settle into the story, get anchored in the present, and care about the characters. That means it's best to keep flashbacks out of the first three chapters of your book. I definitely wouldn't use a flashback in your opening chapter.

Later in the book, a flashback can be a great way to give readers unique insight into your character's past, but even then, I'd suggest you keep it short and make sure there's no other way to reveal a vital piece of backstory.

TIPS FOR HANDLING FLASHBACKS

If you want to use a flashback later in the book, here's how to handle it:

- **Keep the flashback short.** If you interrupt the present story for too long, readers might have problems settling back into it—and might even stop reading altogether.

- **Use a flashback only if it's essential to the plot.** Whatever happened in the past must influence how the character reacts in the present.

- **Make sure your flashback follows a powerful scene in the present.** If a flashback follows a boring scene, readers have no reason to return to the story.

- **Give your protagonist a reason to think about the past.** Build in triggers in the present that make the character remember something from the past. For example, a certain smell or a song could remind them of an event in their childhood.

- **Use signal words that let readers know when you are jumping back in time and returning to the present.** At the start and the end of a flashback, orient readers in time and place immediately. Words such as "back then" or "when she'd been fifteen" indicate that we're stepping back in time, while "now" shows that we are returning to the present.

- **Change verb tense to signal the start and the end of a flashback.** In a novel written in past tense, use the past perfect (e.g., had seen) two or three times when you enter a flashback to indicate that we're entering the past. Writing the entire flashback in the past perfect would be cumbersome, though, so after using it twice, use past tense (e.g., saw) for the rest of the scene. When you're about to jump back to the present, use past perfect once or twice and then resume the story in the present with simple past. Here's an example:

> Sarah put her arms behind her head and looked around her old room. It was still the same worn carpet and the same ugly wallpaper as the last time she'd been here fifteen years ago.
>
> Back then, she had been lying on the bed the way she was now, listening to music, when her father had barged into the room.
>
> "Get downstairs," he had said. "Now!"
>
> Heart hammering, she rolled out of bed and followed him downstairs.
>
> Her father slammed a letter onto the dining room table. "You applied to college without telling me? What about the store?"

Then we'd see the entire conflict between father and daughter playing out, written in past tense. Here's an example that shows you how to switch back into the here and now of the story:

> "If that's how you feel, leave," her father had said, his back to her. "Leave and never come back."

```
"I won't," she had shouted.

Yet here she was, fifteen years later, staring
at the wall of her childhood bedroom.
```

If the story is written in present tense, the flashback should be in past tense.

- **Don't use italics to set off flashbacks.** Italics are hard to read, so you shouldn't use them for longer passages.

- **Be especially careful of info dumps in flashbacks.** Focus on dialogue and action, not on internal monologue, setting description, or other information in flashbacks.

- **Avoid flashbacks within flashbacks.** Within your flashback scene, stay in the present and don't have the character think of things that happened even further back in time.

FRAME STORIES

Frame stories, also called frame narratives, are stories that make use of flashbacks. But unlike the stories we discussed above, where we flash back to the past for just one scene, the flashback takes up most of the story in a frame narrative. Basically, it's a story within a story. Often, the story begins with an older narrator who then tells a story from their past to an audience. The bulk of the story is one long flashback, and we only return to the narrator in the present at the end. You could say the narrator "frames" the main part of the story.

We find frame stories in Homer's *Odyssey* and Mary Shelley's *Frankenstein*. Frame narratives are also used in some movies such as *Titanic*, where an elderly Rose tells a team of treasure hunters about her experiences onboard the Titanic.

Frame stories come with their own drawbacks. For example, since we already know that the narrator survived, that kills part of the tension in adventure or suspenseful stories. Frame narratives are also more limited in their choice of point of view because they have to stick to the narrator's viewpoint. I'd advise you to use it only if you have a very good reason for it.

EXERCISE #70:

- Can you think of a novel in your genre with a well-handled flashback? At which point of the book did the flashback occur? Unless it's a frame story, probably not right at the beginning, right? How did the author handle the transitions into and out of the flashback? If you find any signal words or techniques that might help you, write them down.

EXERCISE #71:

- Look at your own manuscript. Is it a frame narrative? If it is, is this really the most effective structure for your book, or would it work better without the frame? Try it out!
- Are there any flashbacks in your manuscript? If they are in the first few chapters, I strongly urge you to cut them and either use them later in the book or find another way to reveal the backstory. If you have a flashback later in the book, use the checklist above to make sure you handled it well.

28. Flash-forwards —
Why opening with a teaser from later in the book can be tricky

A flash-forward is similar to a flashback, only we're jumping forward in time, not backward. Often, flash-forwards will be used as a prologue. The writer opens the book with a scene that takes place later in the book, then jumps back to the present and shows how the characters got into a certain situation.

Basically, an exciting scene from the middle or the end of a book serves as a hook or teaser that draws readers in.

As with flashbacks and prologues, opening with a flash-forward can be tricky.

THE PROBLEM WITH FLASH-FORWARDS

- **Flash-forwards are often an attempt to cover up a boring opening.** It's as if the author were saying, "Listen, I know the first chapters are awfully dull, but here's a teaser to prove that it will get interesting eventually." But inserting an exciting scene before a boring first chapter doesn't make those first chapters any more interesting. Work on revising your opening chapters instead.

- **Opening with a flash-forward can make the rest of the story feel like a flashback,** which means it comes across like backstory to readers, and that makes it less immediate.

- **Showing readers a scene from later in the book can give away the ending** and kill some of the suspense, if you're not careful.

- **At the beginning of a novel, readers don't yet care about the characters.** The same scene that will have them at the edge of their seats at the end of the book, when they had time to bond with the characters, won't be as effective in chapter 1. That's why flash-forwards seem to work more effectively when used in TV shows, while they are trickier in books. In TV shows, the audience is already familiar with and cares about the characters when they see them in danger in the flash-forward, but that's not the case in a standalone book.

- **Jumping in time can be disorienting and confusing to readers**, just as with flashbacks. Any deviation from the chronological sequence can disrupt the reader's immersion into the story.

- **Flash-forwards delay the inciting incident**, which is the real start of the story. Here's an example:

  Prologue/flash-forward: We get a teaser of Sarah being held at gunpoint.

  Chapter 1: We backtrack to Sarah's ordinary world and see her get ready to go to work. We find out she's a bank clerk.

  Chapter 2: We are introduced to the second main character, Tim, and get a glimpse of his ordinary world. We find out he's a business owner and on his way to drop off money at the bank.

  Chapter 3: We get a flashback to a piece of Sarah's backstory and find out she was having an affair with her manager.

Chapter 4: Just as Tim enters the bank and steps up to the counter, with Sarah behind it, armed bank robbers storm in and take Sarah, Tim, and the bank manager hostage.

The inciting incident—the moment the bank robbery happens—is delayed until chapter 4, which is basically chapter 5 because we also have a prologue. It might have been better to start with chapter 4 and show just a hint of one character's ordinary world before the bank robbery happens. The rest can be filled in later.

So while flash-forwards can work in some stories, I'd advise you not to use them to open your novel—unless you have a really good reason.

TIPS FOR HANDLING FLASH-FORWARDS

If you have decided that you want to use a flash-forward despite the problems they can cause, here are a few tips on how to handle it:

- **Use time markers to orient readers when you are jumping back and forth in time.** For example, at the end of the flash-forward, something such as "Five days earlier" can let readers know that we're now backtracking.

- Just as with flashbacks, **keep flash-forwards brief and powerful.** For example, the *Everest* trilogy by Gordon Korman starts with a flash-forward that is just a few paragraphs long. Book 1 starts with a funeral for a climber on Everest who's missing and presumed dead. Then we jump back to a group of teenagers preparing and then trying to reach the summit. We have to wait until the last pages of book 3 to find out the identity of the teenager who died.

- **Keep the flash-forward strictly in the present of that scene**, without any backstory dumps, flashbacks, or memories of the past.

- **End the flash-forward with a cliffhanger.** You want your readers to wonder not only how characters got to that point, but also how they'll manage to get out of that situation.

- **Make sure the scene that follows the flash-forward is interesting.** If you wrench readers out of a captivating scene and then bore them with a static situation full of info dumps or a slow opening, they are going to stop reading.

- **Be careful not to give away any plot twists or to diminish the suspense.** Show only a fraction of the scene as it later plays out, and don't give away too much.

EXERCISE #72:

- Have you ever encountered a flash-forward opening in a book in your genre? If you haven't, even though you are an avid reader, that might be an indication that they are tricky to pull off in your genre. Think twice before using a flash-forward. If you have encountered books with a flash-forward, did they work? How did the authors pull them off?

EXERCISE #73:

- If you have chosen a flash-forward opening for your novel, study the list of problems flash-forwards can cause. Do you still think this is the best opening for your book? If you do, use the above checklist to make sure it works as effectively as possible.

CONCLUSION —
What to do next

In this book, you've learned a lot about how to structure your story beginning, where to start your book, how to hook your readers and ground them in the story world, and how to avoid the common mistakes that would lead to your beginning being too slow, confusing, misleading, or clichéd.

If you have read each chapter, you should now have a fairly good idea of how to write a great beginning. If you have taken the time to do the exercises at the end of each chapter, you should have a first chapter that draws your readers into your story and makes them want to keep reading. If you haven't yet done the exercises, I urge you to go back and do them now.

But that's really just the starting point. Every newly acquired skill must be practiced. The best advice won't do you any good if you don't incorporate it into your writing. So once you have completed revising the first chapter of your novel, continue with chapter two, chapter three, and the rest of your opening chapters, using the techniques discussed in this book. Some of these techniques can even be incorporated beyond your beginning, in acts 2 and 3 of your book.

Keep revising until you are happy with each scene, and keep coming back to this book for pointers and refreshers.

Once you have revised your manuscript to the best of your ability, your next step should be to get some objective feedback. Find a couple of beta readers willing to read your manuscript and let you know what's working and what isn't. Make sure to ask people who are avid readers in the genre you're writing in. Asking a person who only reads mystery novels to beta read a romance (or the other way around) won't do you much good. Ask them to tell you what kind of questions they were asking as they read, and have them point out the places where they got bored or confused. Use that feedback to further revise your manuscript.

You might also want to keep an eye on how other writers employ these tools. Whenever you read a book, be aware of what pulls you into a story as a reader so that you can use these techniques in your own writing. You could keep a notebook or a file on your computer in which you write down little creative tricks and tips you encounter in the books you read.

Thank you for taking the time to read this book. I hope you found it helpful. If you did, I would appreciate it if you would leave a review where you bought it. Your review might help other writers find this and provide inspiration to those struggling to write a great beginning.

Thank you for your support!

Sandra Gerth

About Sandra Gerth

Sandra Gerth is a writer and an editor who divides her time between writing her own books and helping other writers revise and polish theirs.

She holds a degree in psychology and worked as a psychologist for eight years before transitioning into a career as a full-time novelist—the best job in the world as far as she's concerned.

She earned a certificate in editing from the Academy of German Book Trade and is now the senior editor at Ylva Publishing, a small press that publishes fiction for women who love women.

Under her pen name, Jae, she has published twenty novels and more than two dozen short stories. Her books have won numerous awards and have been #1 best-sellers on Amazon on various occasions.

She's also the author of a series of books for writers, including *Show, Don't Tell* and *Point of View*.

CONNECT WITH SANDRA GERTH

Website: www.sandragerth.com

Other Writers' Guides from Ylva Publishing

www.ylva-publishing.com

Show, Don't Tell

(Writers' Guide Series)

How to write vivid descriptions, handle backstory, and describe your characters' emotions

Sandra Gerth

ISBN: 978-3-95533-750-6

Length: 95 pages (45,000 words)

Show, don't tell is probably the single most-important piece of advice given to writers. But many writers struggle to understand this powerful principle or have difficulty applying it to their own work. Even experienced authors sometimes don't grasp the finer nuances of showing and telling.

In this book, Sandra Gerth draws on her experience as an editor and a best-selling author to show you how to show and tell you when to tell.

Each chapter includes concrete examples and exercises that will hone your writing skills.

Whether you're a novice writer working on your first story or an established author who has already learned the basics of *showing* and *telling*, this book will help you to:

- Grasp the difference between *showing* and *telling*.
- Understand why *showing* is such a powerful tool.
- Spot *telling* in your own manuscript.
- Keep from *telling* what you have already *shown*.
- Avoid the three danger areas of *telling*.
- Describe your characters and your setting in interesting ways.
- Put powerful emotions into your writing.
- Incorporate backstory into your novel without resorting to *telling*.
- Avoid *overshowing* and swamping your readers with too many details.
- Learn when *telling* is actually a good thing.

Point of View
(Writers' Guide Series)

How to use the different POV types, avoid head-hopping, and choose the best point of view for your book

Sandra Gerth

ISBN: 978-3-96324-295-3

Length: 144 pages (23,000 words)

Point of view (POV) is one of the most powerful tools in a writer's kit, but it's also one of the hardest to understand and master.

In this book, Sandra Gerth draws on her experience as an editor and a best-selling author to teach you how to handle point of view in a way that will make your readers identify with your main character, draw them into the story, and keep them captivated until the very last page.

Each chapter includes concrete examples and exercises that will hone your writing skills. Whether you're a novice writer working on your first story or an established author, this book will help you:

- Discover what point of view is and why it's so important
- Understand the different types of point of view such as first-person, third-person, omniscient, and deep POV
- Choose the point of view that works best for your story
- Write a novel from multiple viewpoints without confusing your readers
- Avoid head-hopping and other POV violations that would throw your readers out of the story
- Write internal monologue and take your readers deeply into your character's mind
- Create suspense and tension by using POV techniques
- Let your readers experience events through your main character's eyes to get them emotionally involved in your story

Time Management for Writers
(Writers' Guide Series)

How to write faster, find the time to write your book, and be a more prolific writer

Sandra Gerth

ISBN: 978-3-95533-553-3 (mobi), 978-3-95533-554-0 (epub)
Length: 45,000 words

In the digital age, publishing a book is easier than ever, but finding the time to write a book is becoming harder and harder. With day jobs, family obligations, household chores, and hobbies, many writers struggle to get any writing done.

At the same time, publishers and readers expect writers to publish multiple books every year and to somehow find enough time to market their books through blogging, social media, and networking.

If you are struggling to find enough time to write or don't get much written once you finally do, this book is for you.

Whether you write fiction or nonfiction, this book will help you to:
- Find enough time to write, even if you have a day job,
- Write and publish more books in less time,
- Use rituals to create a powerful writing habit,
- Get your first drafts written more quickly, while still writing well,
- Deal with distractions and interruptions,
- Find your most productive writing routine and environment,
- Use writing challenges to become more productive,
- Discover tools and resources that help you focus on your writing,
- Manage your e-mail in-box in less time,
- Decide how much time to spend writing versus marketing,
- Overcome writer's block and procrastination.

Wrtite Great Beginnings. How to start a novel, hook readers from page one, and avoid common first-chapter problems
© 2020 by Sandra Gerth

ISBN: 978-3-96324-339-4

Also available as e-book.

Published by Ylva Publishing, legal entity of Ylva Verlag, e.Kfr.

Ylva Verlag, e.Kfr.
Owner: Astrid Ohletz
Am Kirschgarten 2
65830 Kriftel
Germany

www.ylva-publishing.com

First edition: 2020

Credits
Edited by Amber Williams
Cover Concept by Streetlight Graphics

Made in the USA
Coppell, TX
09 April 2021

53422790R00121